I0816234

Christ in Our Midst

Daily Lenten Reflections Through Scripture & Gregorian Chant

PARACLETE PRESS
BREWSTER, MASSACHUSETTS

There is none like you among the gods, O Lord,
  nor are there any works like yours.
All the nations you have made shall come
  and bow down before you, O Lord,
  and shall glorify your name.
For you are great and do wondrous things;
  you alone are God.
Teach me your way, O LORD,
  that I may walk in your truth;
  give me an undivided heart to revere your name.
I give thanks to you, O Lord my God, with my whole heart,
  and I will glorify your name forever.
For great is your steadfast love toward me;
  you have delivered my soul from the depths of Sheol.

—*Psalm 86:8–13*

The sacred universe

into which Gregorian chant introduces us

is the world of prayer—

or, if you prefer, of union with God,

which is the ultimate goal of prayer.

—Dom Jacques Hourlier,

Reflections on the Spirituality of Gregorian Chant

Welcome

What a privilege to join you in a Lenten journey. Through a thoughtful collection of chants, Scriptures, meditational readings, and introspective reflections, we hope you will encounter the Holy Trinity in ways that deepen and enrich your faith.

This book begins on Ash Wednesday and ends after a full week of Easter celebrations, launching each reader into a joyous Eastertide. Numbered days are not assigned to daily readings so that readers may utilize this guided devotional journal at any point during the Lenten season. QR codes are conveniently provided throughout the pages to directly connect each reader to poignant chants for personal listening, contemplation, and enjoyment.

In a world filled with noise, stress, and anxiety, the sound of these pure and ancient strains of praise to God can bring otherworldly comfort. May the days ahead be blessed with wonder, renewal, and peace-filled preparation as we join together in hope and expectation on our journey toward Resurrection Sunday.

Alleluia and Amen.

Before you begin . . .

This devotional has been created for you to listen and read, thus fully experiencing the richness of chant throughout Lent—first, engaging with the sound, and second, engaging with the text.

We've included various features to help you navigate the material effectively. There are prompts on each page to either "Scan" or "Listen." Scanning each QR code allows for a complimentary and easy connection to an audio recording of a particular chant. We want you to be absorbed by the sound.

- One chant is provided for Ash Wednesday and each of the three days that lead to the first Sunday of Lent.
- Beginning that first Sunday, one chant is provided for each Sunday of Lent, allowing one chant to carry the theme of meditation for Weeks 1 through 5. On weekdays, the reader should refer to that week's chant through the QR code provided on that day.
- One chant is provided for each day of Holy Week, beginning with Palm Sunday and ending on Easter Sunday.
- One chant appears for Easter Monday and serves as the theme for the rest of Easter Week.

We hope this will open new doors on your faith journey and be an enlivening experience for you during these days of Lent and Easter.

Chant is for Everyone

Meditational chant provides a rhythm of prayer by which we offer praise to God and ponder his Word. The very act of chanting helps us lift our bodies and engage our minds in a way not common to everyday conversation. This devotional is intended to remind readers that the source and meaning of our lives are to be found beyond the mundane tasks that otherwise define our daily schedules. Through chant, we become part of a company of voices worshiping God. When we engage in chant, we enter into eternal time and into the Holy Trinity's presence in a particular, effective manner. We join in the ceaseless round of prayer and praise that flows upward to God from every corner of the world as if incense in a throne room (Rev. 8:3–4).

When we chant the ancient texts in Latin, we are united with others who may speak a modern language different from ours. The choice to use Latin in worship is made not to preserve Gregorian chant like a museum exhibit for the modern world, but rather to plunge ourselves into a current of prayer and praise that will unite and transform us with brothers and sisters around the globe and throughout time.

About the Cantors

Gloriæ Dei Cantores Schola is dedicated to the singing and study of Gregorian chant. Its expertise and experience come from daily chanting of the Liturgy of the Hours as well as the Ordinary and Proper of the Mass at the Church of the Transfiguration in Orleans, Massachusetts. The Schola also conducts chant workshops and performs in concert with Gloriæ Dei Cantores. Years of study with Dr. Mary Berry, CBE, founder of the Schola Gregoriana in Cambridge, England, and the monks of St. Peter's Abbey in Solesmes, France, also contribute to the Schola's passion for Gregorian chant as a vibrant and living form of sung prayer. Gloriæ Dei Cantores Schola has been critically acclaimed in both Europe and the United States for its proper regard for rhythmic flexibility and its sensitivity to both musical and textural phrase.

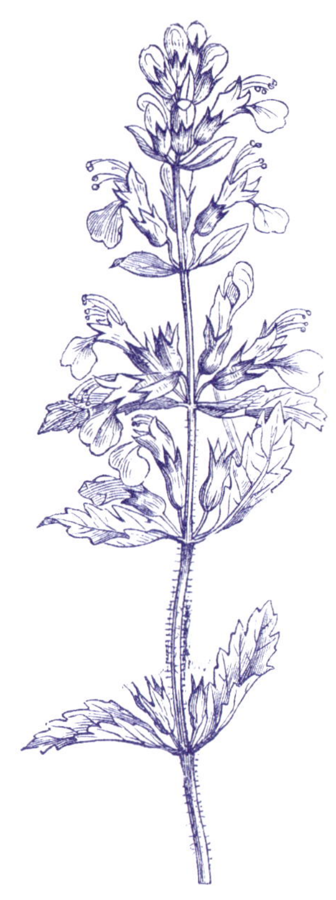

A Brief History of Chant

Gregorian chant is the unique music of Western Christianity. Gregorian chant received its title due to the work of the sixth-century pope Gregory the First (or Saint Gregory the Great), who was renowned for his love of music and his desire to organize chants from diverse traditions to establish a more uniform standard for use in the entire Western region of the Church. Chant is our closest living link with the church of the first centuries. "The first Christians, themselves of Jewish descent, . . . brought into their worship the Jewish custom of chanting aloud the books of the Bible. The melodies they used brought out the meaning of the words. Chanting of the psalms was to become the basis for Christian worship."[1]

In the ninth century, the Holy Roman Emperor Charlemagne joined various strands of spiritual practice—all having their roots in the ancient church—to help solidify his kingdom. As one of the strands, Gregorian chant became a unifying force in Christian worship in an empire that included large portions of Western Europe. Although the Holy Roman Empire crumbled after Charlemagne's death, the form of chant that he promoted continued in practice throughout the West for centuries. During these centuries, monks made two major contributions. First, they organized the chants into an ancient Greek system of eight modes. Second, the monks invented a way to write down notes using markings called *neumes*: In some ways, these markings resemble modern shorthand. In the eleventh century, a system of lines and letters was invented to portray melodies. By the end of the twelfth century, square shapes began to be used to indicate pitch. Once chant music could be written down using the line-and-square-note system, the ancient neumes fell out of use.

1 Mary Berry, *Plainchant for Everyone*, Royal School of Church Music Handbook No. 3 (TSCM, 1979), 3.

The words and lessons of each chant are rooted in Scripture. Those who sing chant in Latin use the same words—and perhaps the same melodies—that have sustained worship for sixty generations of Christians. Gregorian chant as a form of church music has made a resurgence in the eyes and ears of the general public, and many people are finding that the "sacred universe" into which chant introduces us is readily available to them. For the sake of convenience in this offering, both the Latin text and the English translation of each chant are provided.

The Nature of Chant

Chant comes from the aural tradition, meaning everything is passed down through hearing, listening, and imitating. To learn the art of singing chant, it is highly recommended that one listen to chant and allow the music, cadence, and pronunciation of words to sink in. This devotional is intended for readers to listen, absorb, and enjoy the beauty of chant, and then join right in!

Just as in earlier centuries, a novice monk in training for the position of cantor, or choir leader, would invest up to ten years in listening, learning, feeling, and memorizing all the necessary chants for various services. The invention of notation was meant as a reminder—not a teacher. It is essential to first listen with the desire to understand the ebb and flow transmitted from one voice to another's ears. Listening to chants can quickly speak to hearts and spirits.

After listening, one can choose to participate in this unique and profound form of worship. To learn how to start singing chant, we first must look at the notation used in chant. Using lines and notes to represent pitches and their relationship is called *musical notation*. When we look at any piece of chant, we immediately notice that the music looks different from modern notation. The chant neumes, or notes, are known as *square notation*.

Using the QR code provided, listen to *Agnus Dei.* As you listen, hear how the tune follows the line of the music you are looking at. Now try to sing the chant with the music provided via the code.

Scan to Listen to "Agnus Dei"

Agnus Dei

ENGLISH TRANSLATION:

O Lamb of God, Who takes away the sins of the world, give them rest.
O Lamb of God, Who takes away the sins of the world, give them rest.
O Lamb of God, Who takes away the sins of the world, give them everlasting rest.

The scribes who wrote out the notation used quill pens with square tips and, depending on the angle at which they were holding the implement, they were able to make the shapes that we see in the piece of chant above.

The square notes are placed on four lines that go horizontally across the page. We call these lines a *staff*. In modern music, the staff has five lines. Most chant pieces have a moderate range of notes, so a staff with only four lines is used.

One of the differences between square chant notation and modern notation is that square notes represent *relative* pitch, while modern notes represent *absolute* or fixed pitch. The purpose of chant notes is to show the *relationship* between the pitches, not the pitches themselves. You can pick any starting pitch that is comfortable for you, and then sing the rest of the notes relative to that one.

Wherever you sing chant—in your bedroom, in your car, on a walk—you are joining a company of prayerful pilgrims who are speaking to God and listening for his voice. Chant, by its very nature, consists as much in listening as it does in chanting. Whether you are chanting by yourself with pre-recorded audio or if you are chanting with a group, listening is the key for staying on track and moving as one voice. Gregorian chant is poetry of praise in word and song—a language of the prayerful heart.

PRONUNCIATION TIPS WHEN READING LATIN

a as in f**a**ther: Pater, ángelus

e, æ and œ as in pr**e**y: Dómine, exáudi, cælis, cœna

i and y as in the vowel sound in s**ea**: e.g. benedícat, Dóminus, kýrie

i followed by a vowel at the beginning of a word as in **y**es: Iesus, Ioseph, iurávit

o as in r**o**pe: sperábo, orémus

u as in r**u**de: Spíritus, refúgium

au as in **ow**l or c**ow**: lauda, exaudívit

eu as in "**AAY-ooo**": euge, heu

c as in o**k**ay before -a, -o and -u: cadent, cum, corde

c as in pa**tch** before -e and -i: decem, sacrifícium, incípit

ch as in **ch**ris: Christo, chérubim, chorus

g as in **g**as before -a, -o and -u: singuláriter, synagóga

g as in hu**g**e before -e and -i: ángelis, refúgium

h is always silent: hábitat except for two words: mihi (pronounced "**MEE-kee**") and nihil (pronounced "**NEE-keel**")

ph as in **fl**y: Pháraoh

r is aways **rolled**, like an r of Spanish or Italian: refúgium, liberábit, loríca

s as in **s**ee: Deus, spe, requiéscam

th as in **th**yme: thesáuris, thronum

Practice identifying these sounds as you listen to *Jesu Dulcis Memoria* via the QR code provided on page 15.

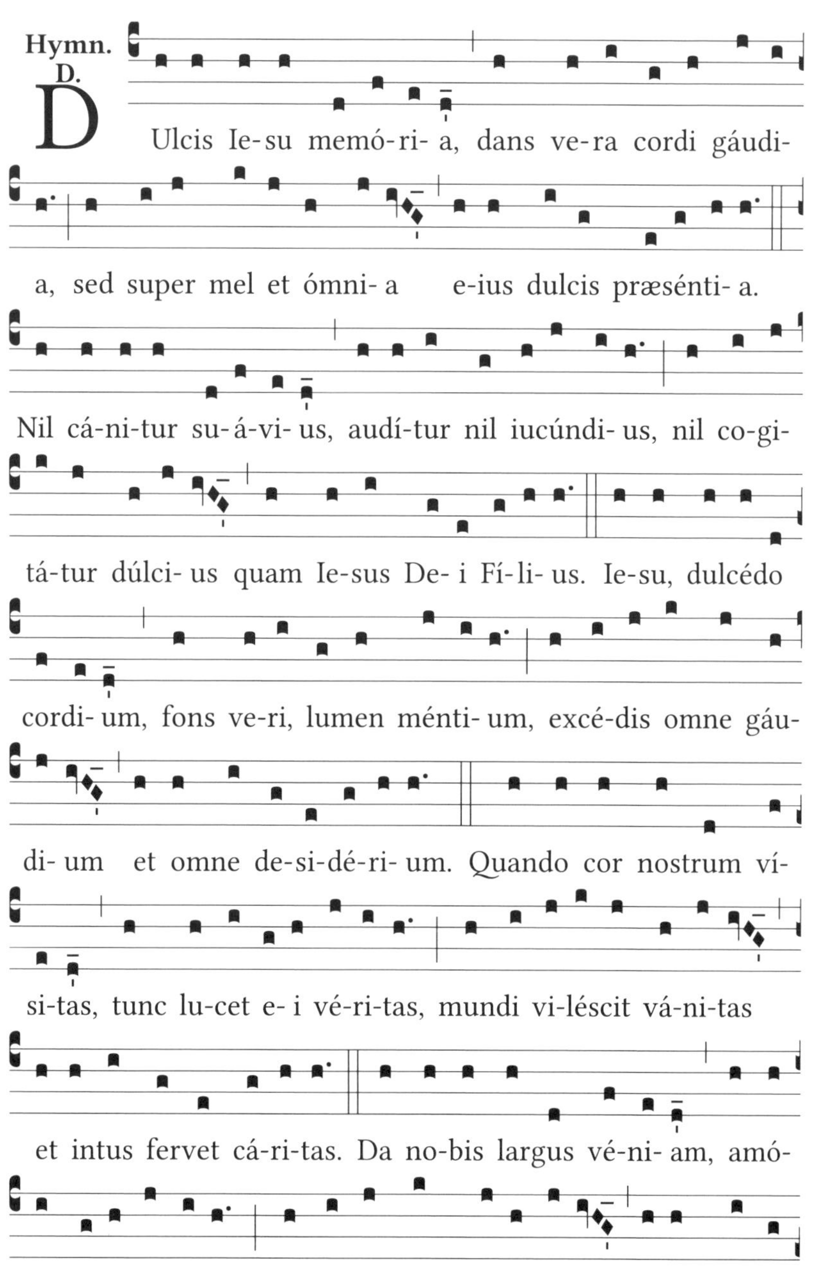
Hymn.
D.
DUlcis Ie-su memó-ri- a, dans ve-ra cordi gáudi-
a, sed super mel et ómni- a e-ius dulcis præsénti- a.
Nil cá-ni-tur su-á-vi- us, audí-tur nil iucúndi- us, nil co-gi-
tá-tur dúlci- us quam Ie-sus De- i Fí-li- us. Ie-su, dulcédo
cordi- um, fons ve-ri, lumen ménti- um, excé-dis omne gáu-
di- um et omne de-si-dé-ri- um. Quando cor nostrum ví-
si-tas, tunc lu-cet e- i vé-ri-tas, mundi vi-léscit vá-ni-tas
et intus fervet cá-ri-tas. Da no-bis largus vé-ni- am, amó-
ris tu- i có-pi- am; da no-bis per præsénti- am tu-am vi-dé-

Scan to Listen to
"Dulcis Jesu Memoria"

Dulcis Jesu Memoria

English translation:

Sweet is the memory of Jesus, giving the heart true joys; but above honey and all things is his sweet presence.

Nothing is sung with more delight, nothing heard with greater joy, nothing pondered more surely than Jesus, the Son of God.

Jesus, sweetness of hearts, fountain of truth, light of souls, you exceed all joy and every desire.

When you visit our heart, then truth shines upon it, the emptiness of the world becomes worthless, and love burns within.

Give us an abundance of pardon, the richness of your love; grant us, by your presence, to see your glory.

We sing praises unto you, the beloved Son,

whom the splendor of the Father and of the Spirit reveals as glorious. Amen.

Ash Wednesday

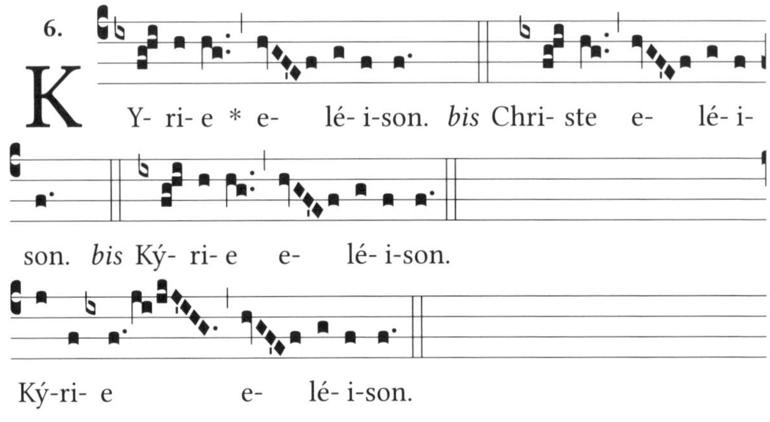

Scan to Listen to
"Kyrie"

Kyrie

English translation:

Lord have mercy,
Christ have mercy,
Lord have mercy.

Note: In Gregorian chant, *bis* is a Latin word meaning "twice." In this recording, it is interpreted to mean the preceding section of chant should be sung twice more.

Ash Wednesday

READ PSALM 51

Have mercy on me, O God.
—Psalm 51:1

We begin our observance of Lent listening to the *Kyrie* from the Requiem Mass and reading Psalm 51, one of the most expressive confessions of sin in the entire Bible. It is sometimes known simply by its opening word in Latin—the *Miserere*: "Have mercy." The brief ascription to this psalm tells of its inspiration: King David has been justly confronted by the prophet Nathan for adultery and murder (2 Sam. 11:1–12:13). "I have sinned against the Lord," answers David. And Psalm 51 is his full confession.

The author of Genesis writes that after disobeying God and eating the forbidden fruit, Adam and Eve "hid themselves from the presence of the LORD God among the trees of the garden" (Gen. 3:8). In their guilt and shame, they ran away from God and took cover. We all recognize this futile maneuver, like a little child who puts his hands over his eyes and says to his mother, "You can't see me." The cause of our guilt may not be as dramatic as David's or Adam's or Eve's, but we still want to "cover up" so we cannot be seen.

Psalm 51 suggests an alternative and much more fruitful response when we find that we have fallen once again. David presents himself honestly and "nakedly" before God. No excuses or evasions. No hiding behind trees or behind hands. Just, "Have mercy." Miserere. Kyrie eleison. Perhaps this is one of the reasons why David is referred to as a man "after [God's] own heart" (1 Sam. 13:14; Acts 13:22).

Notice in Psalm 51 that the psalmist connects God's mercy with things such as joy, gladness, praise, and a new heart. As you begin this season of Lent, name as honestly as you can those places of guilt or shame where you need to know the reality of God's forgiveness.

Thursday After Ash Wednesday

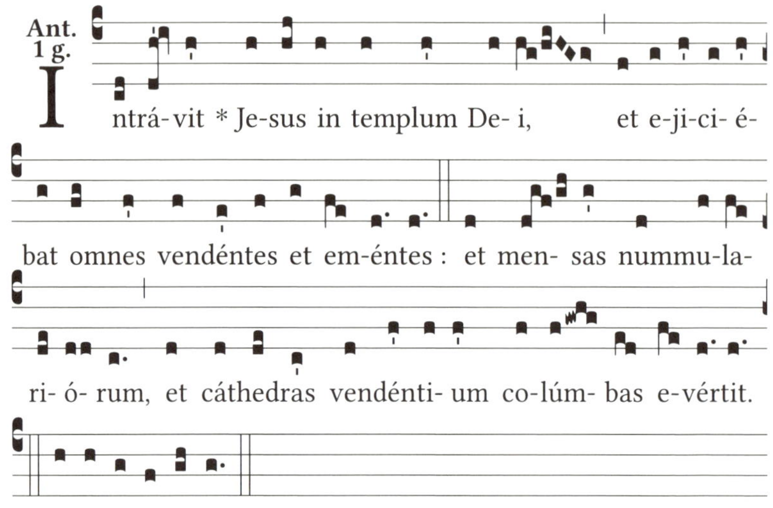

Scan to Listen to
"Intravit Jesus"

Intravit Jesus

English translation:

Jesus went into the temple of God,
and cast out all those who sold and bought,
and he overthrew the tables of the money-changers,
and the chairs of those who sold doves.

Thursday After Ash Wednesday

READ MATTHEW 21:12–13

Then Jesus entered the temple and drove out all who were selling and buying in the temple, and he overturned the tables of the money changers and the seats of those who sold doves.

—Matthew 21:12

Upon his entry into Jerusalem on what we now call Palm Sunday, Jesus's first act was to go to the temple, to "his Father's house" (Lk. 2:49). What Jesus did there would be the preface to all that took place during Holy Week. The city was already in turmoil. But Jesus's righteous anger stunned the religious crowd. It must have been an astonishingly violent few moments—tables and chairs upended, money and goods thrown to the ground, men running into the courtyard. Even if he'd said nothing, Jesus was making an uncompromising pronouncement about the house of the Lord—about whose it was and what it was for.

In truth, it was the cheating money changers and corrupt merchants who had turned things upside down. The tables they set in a place dedicated to the worship of God were laden with selfishness and greed. Their treatment of God's house, but especially of God's people, was a blatant contradiction to the divine priorities of loving God and loving one's neighbor. In actuality, with every table Jesus overturned, he was setting things right side up again.

The Bible teaches us that the human heart is meant to be God's own house. Ever so quietly, though, other priorities slip in, set up their tables, and steal spaces that were meant only for God. By the traditional Lenten practices of prayer, fasting, and almsgiving—sometimes called the three "pillars of Lent"—we endeavor to turn over those cheating tables and clear space for genuine worship. This act may not be as violent as the one Matthew describes, but Lent can be Jesus's opportunity to turn our worlds right side up again.

Identify a table in your heart that is set for something other than God's purposes. What practical act of worship can you take during Lent to turn over this table and receive Jesus's cleansing?

Friday After Ash Wednesday

Resp. 1.

Li- be- ra me * Dó- mi- ne de vi- is infér-
ni, qui portas aére- as confre- gí- sti : et vi-
si-tá- sti inférnum, et de-dísti e- is lu- men,
ut vi-dé-rent te : * Qui e- rant in poe- nis te-
nebrá- rum. ℣. Clamántes et di-
céntes : Adve-ní- sti Redémptor no- ster.

Scan to Listen to
"Libera me"

Libera me

English translation:

Deliver me, O Lord, from the ways of the grave;
You Who have broken down the lofty gates;
and You Who have visited the lower regions,
and given them light, that they may see You:
Those who were in the pain of darkness.
℣. *Crying out and saying: You have come, O our Redeemer.*

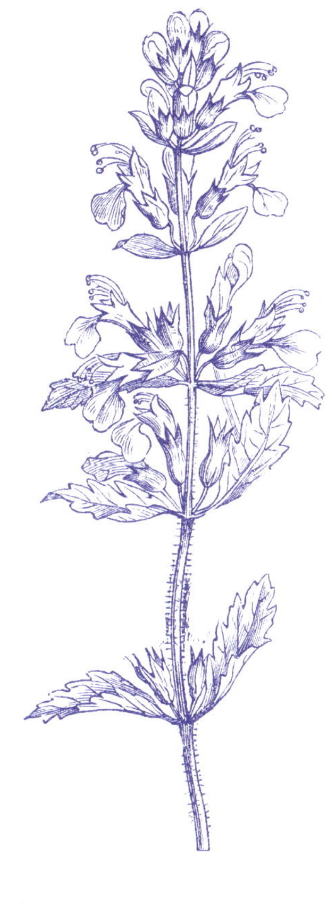

Friday After Ash Wednesday

Read Psalm 107:10–16

Let them thank the Lord *for his steadfast love,*
for his wonderful works to humankind.
For he shatters the doors of bronze and cuts in two the bars of iron.
—Psalm 107:15–16

Based on the words of the Apostles' Creed and the teachings of the early church about Jesus's descent into hell (1 Peter 3:18–20), there is a tradition of sacred art that portrays Jesus in this way: The Son of God stands victoriously upon the broken-down door of hell with its ruined handle and twisted iron hinges; often, Jesus holds a cross in one hand while taking hold of Adam and Eve with the other. In the scene, a multitude of saints watches the unfolding spectacle, and sometimes Satan himself is seen at the very bottom of the picture, writhing in defeat under the very gate behind which he had imprisoned his captives. It is a dramatically mysterious and vividly hopeful image.

This powerful visual is also a colorful representation of today's responsory, *Libera me Domine*, and the selected verses from Psalm 107. Together the image and the impactful words serve as a reminder of where these next days of Lent are taking us. An ancient homily imagines these words spoken by Christ as he breaks down the bars of hell:

> Out of love for you and for your descendants
> I now command all who are held in bondage
> to come forth, all who are in darkness to be
> enlightened, all who are sleeping to arise. I did not
> create you to be held a prisoner in hell. Rise up,
> work of my hands, you who were created in my
> image. Rise, let us leave this place.

What is your hope for this season of Lent? What area of "shadow" has Jesus resurrected? What "captivity" remains in your life that you would like to know the power of Jesus's deliverance?

Saturday After Ash Wednesday

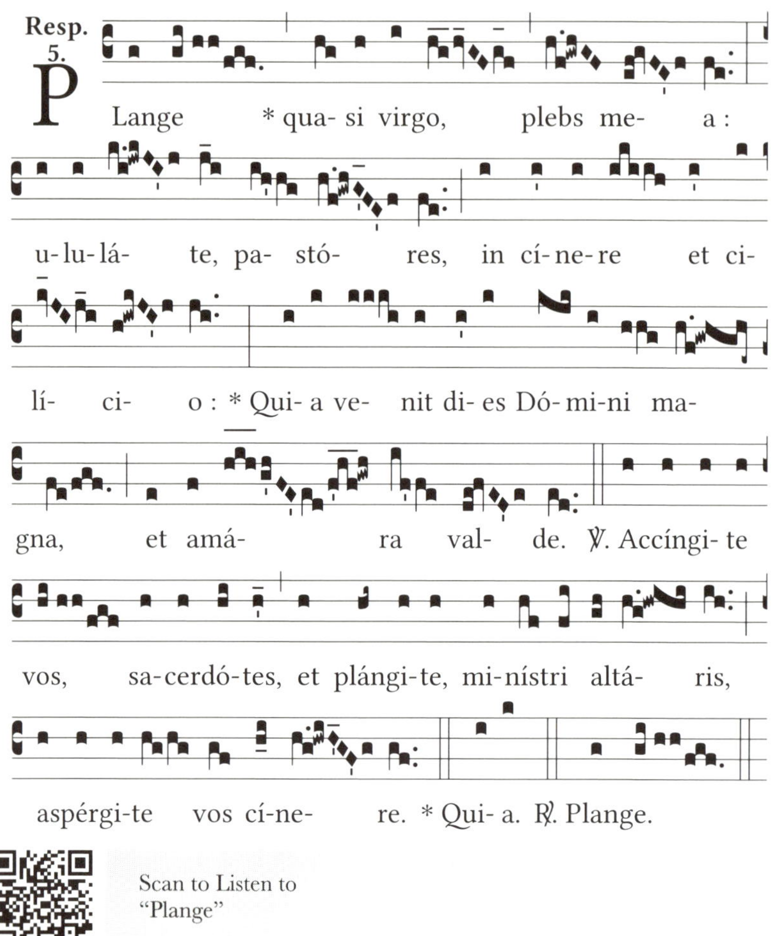

Scan to Listen to "Plange"

Plange

English translation:

Mourn like a virgin, my people; wail, O shepherds, in ashes and sackcloth, for the great day of the Lord is coming, and is extremely bitter.

V. Gird yourselves, you priests, and mourn, you servants of the altar, sprinkle yourselves with ashes.

Saturday After Ash Wednesday

READ JOEL 2:11–17

Yet even now, says the LORD, return to me with all your heart,
with fasting, with weeping, and with mourning; rend your hearts and not your
clothing. Return to the Lord your God, for he is gracious and merciful,
slow to anger, abounding in steadfast love,
and relenting from punishment.

—Joel 2:12–13

In the days of the prophet Joel, a terrible crisis came upon the kingdom of Judah—not an uncommon one, but a particularly devastating one for a nation whose well-being depended primarily on agriculture. A devastating infestation of locusts ravaged the land and caused a widespread famine. "What the cutting locust left, the swarming locust has eaten" (Joel 1:4). Joel's point is not a description of various species of locusts but of the utter devastation left in the wake of these swarms. They left nothing to harvest, and then went on their voracious way—"nothing escapes them" (Joel 2:3).

While lamentation is a fitting response to such a catastrophe—"Wail, O shepherds," says today's responsory—Joel says that repentance is fitting as well. This may be a difficult concept for our modern minds, but we have to remember that it was (and still is) the vocation of the prophet to discern the deeper purposes of God amongst world events. God had not abandoned the people with whom he was in covenant, despite what things looked like. They, in fact, had abandoned God.

And what is God's response to the infidelity of his chosen people? "Return to me," says the Lord; "Who knows whether he will not turn and relent and leave a blessing behind him?" (Joel 2:12, 14). In truth, the call to *repent* has always been an invitation to *return*.

This is why these verses from Joel are read every Ash Wednesday, as an invitation to the observance of Lent. Perhaps this is a good time to also remember the promised coming of the Holy Spirit found a few verses later, in Joel 2:28–29, which is read every Pentecost. God's *invitation* and *promise* stand like two bookends to the Lenten and Easter season.

What circumstances in your life might God be asking you to ponder more deeply than surface level this Lent?
In what way might God be inviting you to "return" to him?

Sunday of the First Week of Lent

Scan to Listen to
"Amen dico vobis"

Amen dico vobis

English translation:

Amen, I say to you;
what you have done to one of my smallest ones, you have done to me;
come, you blessed ones of my Father,
take the kingdom prepared for you from the beginning of time.

Responsory Verse:
Eternal rest grant them, O Lord,
and may perpetual light shine upon them.

Sunday of the First Week of Lent

READ MATTHEW 25:31–46

"Come, you who are blessed by my Father, inherit the kingdom prepared for you from the foundation of the world. Truly I tell you, just as you did it to one of the least of these brothers and sisters of mine, you did it to me."

—Matthew 25:34, 40

Three words in today's chant piece, taken from the Gospel of Matthew, call for our attention:

Come—This is a different *come* than the one heard by the disciples when Jesus first called them. Yes, that *come* was an invitation, but it was also an imperative. It was a commanding call to "Come, follow me." In Jesus's parable, the *come* spoken by the gloriously reigning Son of Man is now a greeting. The solemn *come* that started the saints on their journey becomes the joyful *come* that welcomes them home.

Take—Though the Latin *possidete* can be translated as "take" or "take possession of," it can also mean "inherit," which is the word used in many Bible translations of this verse. In his letter to the Romans, Paul writes that, if we are children of God, then we are also his heirs and fellow heirs with his Son (Rom. 8:17). God means to pass on everything to his family. Each of us is his named beneficiary.

Prepared—"I go and prepare a place for you," Jesus told his disciples (John 14:2–3). We might say that God has been planning a long time for the return of his sons and daughters. Like a careful and generous host, he has taken note of every detail, as if he is about to welcome the most important people he has ever had into his home.

On Ash Wednesday, we are reminded of our inescapable mortality: "You are dust, and to dust you shall return." Today, we are reminded that dust was never meant to be our eternal destiny.

Who has passed on from your life that is an example of one of the sheep at Jesus's right hand? What do you most admire about him/her? Take a moment to give thanks to God for that person.

Monday of the First Week of Lent

READ ISAIAH 58:6–9

Is not this the fast that I choose: to loose the bonds of injustice, to undo the straps of the yoke, to let the oppressed go free, and to break every yoke? Is it not to share your bread with the hungry and bring the homeless poor into your house; when you see the naked, to cover them and not to hide yourself from your own kin?

—Isaiah 58:6–7

Listen. 

Around the time of Lent we often talk a good deal about "giving up" something. As Lent approaches we sometimes ask one another, "What are you giving up for Lent?" As the days of Lent pass, we wonder, "I don't know if I can really give this up for another four weeks!" And when Lent is over, we might say, "Well, I made it. But I'm not sure I can give that up again next year." "Giving up" something for Lent has become the modern-day expression for observing some form of a fast, and fasting has always been one of the pillars of this season of penitence and preparation (more about this later).

Like all religious practices, fasting has its inherent risks, as Jesus warned his disciples: "Beware of practicing your righteousness before others in order to be seen by them" (Matt. 6:1). He specifically cautioned against showing off or over-dramatizing the rigors of one's abstinences for the sake of impressing others (see Matt. 6:16–18).

Never mind others. Least of all is *God* impressed with our fasting. "What good is fasting," asks the prophet Isaiah, "if you ignore the needs of the poor or turn your face from the beggar?" Or if, as the chant piece reminds us, you do not care for one of God's "smallest ones." The real "fast" that God will honor is to abstain from withholding, to go without selfishness, and to sacrifice stinginess. Perhaps the real question we should be asking ourselves for Lent is not "what am I going to give up?" but rather, "what am I going to *give*?"

How do these passages impact your view of "the least of these"?
What might you give this Lent?

Tuesday of the First Week of Lent

Read the Responsory Verse

Eternal rest grant them, O Lord,
and may perpetual light shine upon them.

Listen. 

Before we consider further passages from the Psalms that relate to this week's chant text—Jesus's parable of the sheep and goats—let's look at the verse that is attached to this antiphon. The Latin word *requiem* means "rest." We recognize *Requiem* as the name given to the entire rite, or ceremonial act, for the burial of the dead. The concept is taken from the book of 2 Esdras: "Therefore I say to you, O nations that hear and understand, 'Wait for your shepherd; he will give you everlasting rest, because he who will come at the end of the age is close at hand. Be ready for the rewards of the kingdom, because perpetual light will shine on you forevermore'" (2 Esdras 2:34–35).

Everlasting rest and perpetual light—these are the promised blessings in store for those who follow Christ to the end of their earthly pilgrimage. In the New Testament, the writer to the Hebrews likens heaven to the Sabbath day when God rested from his work in creation and to the Promised Land when the Israelites rested after their journey through the wilderness (see Heb. 3–4). And the apostle John's vision of heaven describes a city where there is no more darkness or night, no more mourning or crying, where the Lamb of God shines like a lamp and the glory of God gives everlasting brightness.

For centuries, this verse has served as a prayer for those who have died. As we make our way through Lent, we remember those who have gone before us, and we entrust them to God's eternal embrace with the hope that we, too, shall find our way to the glorious presence of our Savior.

Imagine entering into Jesus's presence. What emotions and thoughts fill your mind? Write a prayer of gratitude for Christ's invitation to share in his eternal light.

Wednesday of the First Week of Lent

READ PSALM 41:1–3

Happy are those who consider the poor;
the LORD delivers them in the day of trouble.
—Psalm 41:1

Listen. 

One of the traditional readings at the beginning of Lent is the Beatitudes found in Matthew 5:1–12. During his Sermon on the Mount, Jesus provides a commonly repeated list saying, "Blessed are . . .," and this text, in part, is a map of the moral high ground to which Jesus calls his followers. Reading over the Beatitudes, anyone can quickly conclude that we are not capable of navigating this calling apart from him. That, too, is part of the essential meaning of Lent—reliance on Christ.

The opening verse of Psalm 41 is also a "beatitude," one with which Jesus was no doubt intimately familiar. The condition set for happiness, favor, and even good health and divine protection is a heart that considers the needs of the poor. Someone has described this as a circle of grace: The flow of divine love we receive from God only transpires as we make space for it by giving it away to others. A full vessel that has no spout for emptying itself can never be refilled.

Giving of ourselves is certainly a fundamental moral teaching that Lent highlights for us every year, as with this week's chant piece. But it is also more than that. Psalm 41:9 points to the greatest act of self-emptying on behalf of "the poor" that the world has ever known: "Even my close friend in whom I trusted, who ate of my bread, has lifted the heel against me." The circle of grace begins here and ends on the cross.

What would it mean for you to "consider the poor"?
Where might your own full vessel need to be unstoppered?

Thursday of the First Week of Lent

READ PSALM 72:11–14; 18–19

He has pity on the weak and the needy
and saves the lives of the needy.
—Psalm 72:13

Listen. 

The text for this week's chant piece is taken from the parable of the sheep and the goats (Matt. 5:31–46), in which Jesus describes the Son of Man returning at the end of the age, accompanied by his heavenly entourage and seated upon "his glorious throne." At the appointed hour, judgment will come upon all the peoples of the earth. While the closing verses of Psalm 72 may have been prayed at earlier coronations in the house of David, the words seem to be a fitting song in homage to the King of kings: "Blessed be his glorious name forever; may his glory fill the whole earth. Amen and Amen." They are particularly fitting for the Son of Man because this King's right to take the seat of judgment is founded upon his willingness to have first taken the seat of sacrifice.

This brings to mind the style of crucifix known as *Christus Rex*—Christ the King. In such images, Jesus is clothed in royal or priestly garments with a crown upon his head. Even as his arms are outstretched as if he is being crucified, he seems to stand painlessly, regally, and victoriously. The cross itself seems to be his throne.

If Psalm 72 can be a depiction of "Christus Rex," it is because the sovereign described in these verses is also a savior. The needy, the poor, and the helpless are so much more than his subjects. It is a mystery beyond our understanding that, in his sight, their blood is no less precious than his own (v. 14). *Our* blood is no less precious than his own.

What words would you use in prayer today to describe your Sovereign?
What words would you use to describe your Savior?

Friday of the First Week of Lent

Read Psalm 16:5–11

The Lord is my chosen portion and my cup; you hold my lot.
The boundary lines have fallen for me in pleasant places;
I have a goodly heritage.
—Psalm 16:5–6

Listen. 

Preaching to the pilgrims gathered in Jerusalem on the day of Pentecost, the apostle Peter declared that the One who had been crucified and killed by human hands had been marvelously raised up again by the mighty hand of God. Peter heard in Psalm 16 the voice of Christ, so he quoted words that would have been familiar to his listeners stated in Acts 2:27–28: "For you will not abandon my soul to Hades or let your Holy One experience corruption. You have made known to me the ways of life; you will make me full of gladness with your presence." Like Peter, we can imagine Jesus praying these verses as he descends into death or singing them as he rises again from the grave.

This week's chant piece is often heard during a funeral liturgy at the time of communion. The bread of life and the cup of salvation are the fruit borne of Jesus's resurrection and the divine promise of our own. In this context, the psalmist gives us words to pray as we eat and drink: "The Lord is my chosen portion and my cup." Psalm 16 becomes our own prayer of hope and confidence as we follow our Lord through these coming weeks of Lent, through the Passion, to the cross, and out from the grave. For "we know that the one who raised Jesus will also raise us with Jesus and will present us with you in his presence" (2 Cor. 4:14).

What feelings surface when you contemplate a time when you have felt abandoned? How does the idea of the Lord being your portion encourage you or challenge you?

Saturday of the First Week of Lent

Read Psalm 37:1–22

But the meek shall inherit the land
and delight themselves in abundant prosperity.
—Psalm 37:11

Listen. 

When Jesus included a beatitude for the meek in the Sermon on the Mount—"Blessed are the meek, for they will inherit the earth"—it's likely he had Psalm 37:11 in mind. The whole of the psalm appears to be a self-exhortation to "trust in the Lord" in the face of the success and wealth of evildoers. It seems to address the ageless question put before God by the empty-handed: Why do the wicked prosper? "That's too short-sighted a question," the psalmist says. "The wicked will eventually get their fair share . . . but so also will the meek."

Meekness often gets a bad rap. It carries with it a sense of powerlessness and seems to describe someone who can be easily manipulated or taken advantage of. As with other characteristics like gentleness or lowliness, the very word feels a bit uncomfortable, and even distasteful in a world where power is pursued and often worshiped. But let's remember how Jesus described himself in this world—a world he came into to overcome (John 16:33; 2 Cor. 10:1) and whose tables he turned upside-down—"I am gentle and humble in heart" (Matt. 11:29). The strength found in being meek is that the meek do not assert their own agenda but nonetheless undoubtedly trust in God's will. It is not in a meek person's strength, but in their submissive spirit toward God's authority, that impact is felt.

In the traditional Latin funeral liturgy, a final antiphon, *In Paradisum*, is sung as the body of the deceased is borne from the church: "May the angels lead you into paradise; may the martyrs receive you at your arrival and lead you to the holy city Jerusalem." Remember who "wins" in the end.

Where do you need to trust in the Lord for his glory and your faith development? What does being meek have to do with trust?

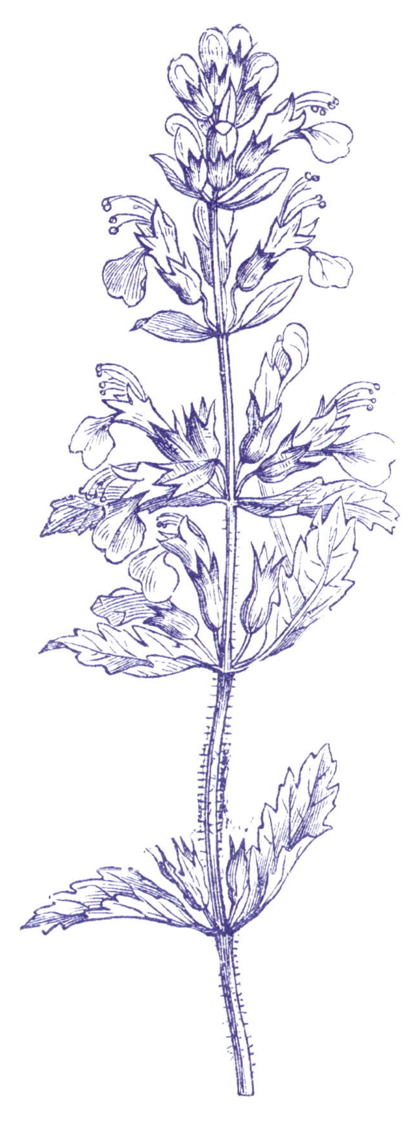

Sunday of the Second Week of Lent

Scan to Listen to
"Visionem"

Visionem

English translation:

The vision which you have seen,
you will tell to no one
until the Son of man rises from the dead.

Sunday of the Second Week of Lent

READ MATTHEW 17:1–9

He was transfigured before them, and his face shone like the sun, and his clothes became bright as light.
—Matthew 17:2

Jesus's Transfiguration, the subject of this week's chant, is one of the most extraordinary and mysterious events recorded in the Gospels (see Mark 9:2–9; Luke 9:28–36). The healing miracles, walking on water, multiplying the loaves and fish, even raising the dead—these were all astonishing wonders, and more than enough to make one ask, "Who is this man Jesus?" But that's just the point. In each case, Jesus appeared to be an ordinary man who could *do* extraordinary things. On the Mount of Transfiguration, however, Jesus *himself* was shown differently from any man Peter, James, and John had ever seen.

All three Gospel accounts agree about what Jesus looked like, though they use different words to describe his indescribable appearance. Matthew says that Jesus's face shone like the sun and his clothes became white as light; Mark says that Jesus's garments glistened more whitely than any bleach could have made them; Luke says that Jesus's countenance changed and his clothes appeared dazzling white. Each writer seems to search for a way to explain not what Jesus did, but what Jesus looked like—white, brilliant, shining, bright as the sun! Mark says that Jesus was "transfigured."

This was no ordinary man who now stood before them. No doubt something in their hearts told them who they were looking at, but if they still wondered how their rabbi could appear this way, the answer came from a voice: "This is my Son, the Beloved; . . . listen to him." It was then, writes Matthew, that Peter, James, and John fell on their faces in awe and wonder.

Read Matthew's account of the Transfiguration aloud, as if to a small group of people gathered around you. What words or phrases are impressed on you?

Monday of the Second Week of Lent

Read Psalm 97

Clouds and thick darkness are all around him;
righteousness and justice are the foundation of his throne.
—Psalm 97:2

Listen. 

Psalms 93–99 are a collection of psalms written in honor of God's reign over all the earth. The language is celebratory and worshipful, and it sometimes draws on dramatic imagery from pivotal events in Israel's history. For example, when the composer of Psalm 97 pictured God surrounded by "clouds and thick darkness," everyone who heard these words would immediately recognize their meaning. It was a pillar of cloud that led the people of Israel through the wilderness and settled on the tabernacle they erected along the way (Exod. 13:21; 40:34); a cloud covered the mountain where Moses met with God and heard his voice (Exod. 19:16–20; 24:15–18); and, when Solomon dedicated the temple in Jerusalem, the cloud was so thick that the priests could not perform their service (1 Kgs. 8:10–12). Because of these events, the cloud in Israel's history has meant not so much that God is hidden, but that God is *present*.

From these events, we see why Psalm 97 is sung with this week's chant. All three Gospel accounts of the Transfiguration tell us of a cloud that engulfed the disciples, and from that cloud they heard the voice of God. No wonder they fell to the ground. What if the darkness that seems to hide God from us is the very place out of which God intends to speak to us? What if the clouds that sometimes descend into our lives really are "the dust of his feet" (Nahum 1:3)?

What are the "clouds" in your life?
How might God be speaking to you through them?

Tuesday of the Second Week of Lent

READ PSALM 77:11–20

Your lightnings lit up the world;
the earth trembled and shook.
—Psalm 77:18

Listen. 

On the Mount of Transfiguration, Jesus shone like the sun; his robes became dazzling white; and, according to Matthew, the cloud that overshadowed the disciples was bright with light. While exiled on the island of Patmos (his punishment for preaching the gospel), the apostle John was given a vision of heaven that began with God's throne. He found language to describe the glorious brilliance of what he saw, including the flashes of lightning bursting forth from the throne (Rev. 4:5). This is the same revelation given to the prophet Ezekiel, who envisioned God's throne appearing out of a great cloud that shone with brightness and flashed forth with lightning (see Ezek. 1). And it was what the Israelites witnessed from the foot of the mountain where Moses brought them to "meet God" (Exod. 19:16–17).

John was writing to persecuted Christians. Ezekiel was prophesying among his fellow exiles. And the people of Israel were making their way through the wilderness to a homeland that was yet to be seen. In every case, bolts of lightning seem to indicate that "the light shines in the darkness" (John 1:5). Clouds of uncertainty, confusion, and even suffering—all of these heavenly images, including the psalmist's, affirm the same message: The Lord reigns.

Those of us in the northern hemisphere enjoy the connection between the season of Lent and the growing daylight that marks spring's arrival. Ironically, this season, which is connected with so many dark memories—Jesus fasting in the wilderness, his betrayal, abandonment, suffering, and death—holds the hope of an emerging light that can never be hidden as we make our way through the wilderness to an eternal homeland that is yet to be seen.

In what circumstances in your life do you need to trust that God's light will prevail? Where do you need to confess: "The Lord reigns"?

Wednesday of the Second Week of Lent

READ PSALM 27

"Come," my heart says, "seek his face!"
Your face, LORD, do I seek. Do not hide your face from me.
—Psalm 27:8–9

Listen. 

"The LORD is my light and my salvation; whom shall I fear?" (Ps. 27:1). These are not the words of someone cowering in a dark corner. The psalmist may be faced with approaching danger, but the face he turns to is God's. "Your face, LORD, do I seek."

"Face-to-face" in any relationship first requires the desire for closeness, then a trust that the other wants this as well, and, finally, the act of looking one another in the eye—of seeing and being seen. Is this a friendship, an intimacy, that is possible with the Maker and Ruler of the universe?

The unconcealed glory of God is too much for human eyes to take in. Moses found this out on a mountain in the Sinai desert (see Exod. 33:17–23). We get a taste of this when we are captured by something so intensely beautiful that it brings an ache to the heart. What if that beauty was ten thousand times ten thousand times stronger . . . and brighter?

On the Mount of Transfiguration, the disciples saw the countenance of the Son of God, whose face shone like the sun. Years later, John would declare, "We have seen his glory" (John 1:14). "Veiled in flesh the Godhead see," wrote Charles Wesley in his beloved Christmas carol "Hark, the Herald Angels Sing." Jesus Christ presents to us the face of God in a form humanity can withstand, so to speak, even if it may still smart. Join with the psalmist in praying, "Your face, Lord, do I seek."

At what moments in life have you felt the glory of the Lord around or near you? How can you engage with the Lord "face-to-face" this week?

Thursday of the Second Week of Lent

Read Luke 9:28–37

They appeared in glory and were speaking about his exodus, which he was about to fulfill in Jerusalem.
—Luke 9:31

Listen. 

Of all the possible companions who could have stood with Jesus on the Mount of Transfiguration, why Moses and Elijah? Much has been written about their presence, which helps us to understand the multifaceted meaning of this mysterious event. As representatives of the Law (Moses) and the Prophets (Elijah), these two men point to Jesus as God's promised fulfillment of both. They stand as heavenly witnesses to God's Word made flesh, the One in whom God's unfaltering desire for the salvation of humanity is fulfilled. Each represents God's covenant relationship with his people, the covenant that was made on Mount Sinai when God provided the Ten Commandments and that was renewed through the voice of every Old Testament prophet. And, interestingly, neither Moses nor Elijah died in the traditional sense (see Deut. 34:5–6; 2 Kgs. 2:11). So, perhaps their presence in the company of Jesus—the Resurrection and the Life—also answers any speculation about their ultimate destiny. Heaven is real, and they are with God—plain and simple.

While all three Gospel accounts tell us of their appearance, only Luke tells us that Moses and Elijah were talking with Jesus about something. The Greek text is unambiguous—they were speaking about Jesus's *exodus* from Jerusalem. Just consider all the meaning that is contained in this word—all the history, the struggle, the miracles, the sacrifice, and the promise. Moses and Elijah knew that Jesus was about to pass from earth in a similar way again, although he would be radically victorious. The face on the mountain that shone in glory was about to pass through the valley and go to Jerusalem (Lk. 9:51).

What does Jesus's resolute will to face those who opposed him in Jerusalem tell us about what it means to be his disciple? What encouragement does it specifically provide regarding your own discipleship?

Friday of the Second Week of Lent

Read Mark 9:2–8

Then Peter said to Jesus, "Rabbi, it is good for us to be here; let us set up three tents: one for you, one for Moses, and one for Elijah."
—Mark 9:5

Listen. 

Yes, the apostle Peter was afraid. And yes, even when he didn't know what to say—*especially* when he didn't know what to say—Peter blurted out the first thing that came to his mind. Sometimes Peter is faulted for his unfiltered reaction to a sight that was at the same time both transfixing and terrifying. The thought is that he wanted to extend the mystical experience—"Let's put up tents for each of you so we can stay here and enjoy this all night." Peter loved Jesus, we know, and no doubt he would have liked being in his Master's glorified presence as long as possible. But Peter's words may have been more than a self-interested desire couched in an offer to provide shelter for Jesus and his heavenly companions.

The cloud, a central character in all three accounts of the Transfiguration, is understood to be God's *Sh'kinah*, God's *glory* or, as sometimes translated, God's *dwelling*. When Moses entered this cloud on Mount Sinai, one of the first instructions God gave him was that the people should "make me a sanctuary so that I may dwell among them" (Exod. 25:8). In John's vision of eternity, he heard that God intended to make his dwelling with his people, a building that he began when "the Word became flesh and dwelt among us" (John 1:14, RSV). Is it possible that Peter, a simple Jewish Galilean fisherman, may have perceived the vision before him fairly accurately? And that, even if refused, Peter's first instinct to build something may have been spot on?

What does it mean to you that Jesus wants to be in your presence? How can your body be a temple for God's dwelling?

Saturday of the Second Week of Lent

READ MATTHEW 17:1–9

As they were coming down the mountain, Jesus ordered them, "Tell no one about the vision until after the Son of Man has been raised from the dead."
—Matthew 17:9

Listen. 

We conclude this week's devotions by returning to the text of the antiphon we began with on Sunday. Jesus and his three chosen visionaries are coming down the mountain. Moses and Elijah are gone, the bright cloud has lifted, Jesus appears to them as he has always appeared, and "normal" life resumes. That would be a hard enough transition from the grandeur they had just experienced. But Jesus seems to move them even a step further from the glory of the mountaintop. "Keep this to yourselves," he tells them. These were Jesus's followers, witnesses to his words and deeds, the future evangelists of his kingdom. What could explain his order that they tell no one this good news?

As we have already seen, Luke tells us that from this point on, Jesus's eyes are set upon the road to Jerusalem, where he will be delivered over for trial and execution (see John 17:1). The glory to which he is first calling his disciples is not the glory of the Transfiguration but the glory of the Cross. Might Jesus have been saying to Peter, James, and John: "There's more to come. I do not want people following me because they think I am a King, though you have seen that I am, but because they know I am a Savior, which none of you have yet seen. When the whole story is finished, then this secret between you and me will be for everyone. Then, you can shout it from the housetops!"

The writer of Ecclesiastes says that there is "a time to keep silent and a time to speak" (3:7). How do we know the difference? How do you discern the Lord's instructions?

Sunday of the Third Week of Lent

Scan to Listen to
"Accepit ergo"

Accepit ergo

English translation:

And Jesus then took the loaves,
and when he had given thanks,
he distributed to the people as they sat there.

Sunday of the Third Week of Lent

READ JOHN 6:1–14

Then Jesus took the loaves, and when he had given thanks
he distributed them to those who were seated;
so also the fish, as much as they wanted.
—John 6:11

The antiphon chosen for this week, though brief, is rich with meaning, and our reflections over the coming days will look at the various ways it is presented in the Bible in both the Old and New Testaments. The music itself has a simple clarity, for the most part assigning one note to each syllable, as if to say, "Listen carefully, for the words I bear are more important than I."

The story of Jesus's feeding thousands of people with a meager few loaves of bread and a couple of fish is recorded in all four Gospels. That in itself says something about the significance of this miracle. This antiphon, taken from a single verse of John's account, is sung in the heart of Lent. In the season that recalls Jesus's forty days of fasting alone—Matthew says of Jesus, "he was famished"—we sing of his feeding the multitude—who John says, ate "as much as they wanted."

Jesus *took* and he *distributed*, and between both of these actions, he *gave thanks*. Thus the recipe for life-giving Bread was first written. In the *eucharistia*, the Greek word for "thanksgiving," Jesus gives his very self as food and drink to the hungry and thirsty. When he gave thanks for and broke bread on a hillside overlooking the Sea of Galilee, Jesus was preparing for a later meal. So, when the crowd came to him looking for more, he looked at them and said, "I am the bread of life" (John 6:35).

The feeding of the multitudes is one of the only miracles recorded in all four Gospels, aside from the Resurrection. Why do you think this event is so impactful? What does it mean to feast on Jesus, the Bread of Life?

Monday of the Third Week of Lent

READ 2 KINGS 4:38–44

They ate and had some left, according to the word of the LORD.
—2 Kings 4:44

Listen. 

There are obvious similarities between Elisha's miraculous feeding of the men of Gilgal and Jesus's feeding the multitude along the Sea of Galilee. Not the least of these is that in both cases, what began as a patent undersupply of food was transformed into abundance enough for leftovers. The story of Elisha records two other remarkable elements.

First, verse 38 tells us that there was a famine in this region. In a land so dependent upon agriculture yet given so often to lack of rainfall, famine was all too common. At such times, meager rations might need to last for days, and survival might depend on making the most out of the very least, which is exactly what happened. As it so often does, the miracle of God's plenty appeared in the midst of human poverty. This has always been the plotline in the story of divine grace.

A second noteworthy element of the story is the source of the food that was brought to Elisha. Verse 42 records that a man came from a distant village (a place apparently not suffering famine), bringing with him the first fruits of his crops. It was a law of Israel that before any other part of the harvest was to be enjoyed or stored, a portion was to be given to God with prayer and thanksgiving (see Lev. 23:9–14). This was the portion that the man gave to Elisha and that, in turn, Elisha gave away to others—with miraculous results!

Even in a time of famine—especially in a time of famine—"give and it shall be given to you" still holds true.

What "first fruit" are you willing to give during Lent that God may use for the blessing of others?

Tuesday of the Third Week of Lent

READ PSALM 107:4–9

For he satisfies the thirsty, and the hungry he fills with good things.
—Psalm 107:9

Listen. 

The various people described in Psalm 107 are all in dire need of one kind or another and, even if not literally, the condition of our own souls from time to time may be read in these vivid images. The opening verses speak of a people lost in the wilderness, fainting for want of food and water. Drawing from the history of the people of Israel (see Exod. 16:13–18), the psalmist reminds us that God is still "satisfying the thirsty" and "filling the hungry," words echoed in the Virgin Mary's song as she bore the "Bread of Life" in her own body: "He has filled the hungry with good things" (Lk. 1:53). Recall the text of Sunday's Scripture, telling us that Jesus fed the multitude "as much as they wanted." The measure of their need determined the measure of their fill. God's goodness did not, and *does* not, run out.

From everyone whose need is met by the mercy of God, the psalmist calls for thanksgiving—"Let them thank the LORD" (v. 8)—which is the only proper response to God's goodness. There is no other offering to be given in answer to grace. So, perhaps one way to approach the meaning of these early verses of Psalm 107 is to consider the closing verse: "Let those who are wise pay attention to these things and consider the steadfast love of the LORD" (v. 43). The wise person will pay attention to what God has done, for remembrance of God's previous loving acts provokes trust in present times of need and always spawns thanksgiving. The hungry heart becomes a grateful heart.

Recall a situation when God provided for you. How can remembering that experience be of help to you in a current time of need?

Wednesday of the Third Week of Lent

Read Psalm 145:15–16

The eyes of all look to you, and you give them their food in due season. You open your hand, satisfying the desire of every living thing.
—Psalm 145:15–16

Listen. 

Continuing with the theme of God's faithful and abundant provision, which we hear in this week's antiphon, these two verses from Psalm 145 paint a picture of our utter dependence upon his faithfulness (something that will be illustrated even further in tomorrow's reading). Our need for God—*"the eyes of all look to you"*—and for what he gives—*"you open your hand"*—is not something we choose, any more than a child chooses to depend on her parents. It is our natural condition as creatures who are made and sustained by the hand of God. "In him we live, and move, and have our being," writes the apostle Paul (Acts 17:28).

The eyes of all look to you. The psalmist imagines every creature under heaven, with eyes turned upward, looking to God for food and drink. The direction we "look" toward is determined by what we know to be the source of what we need. Looking elsewhere leads only to wanting more, or even comparing our state with that of those around us.

You open your hand. The open hand of God is the image of heavenly generosity and grace. God is neither stingy nor calculating with his gifts. His hand is as open to us as is his heart.

Psalm 145 is entitled "A Song of Praise" (the only such psalm with this title), and it is the first of the final six psalms, all of which are sustained poetry in praise of God. When God is known—or *experienced*—as the maker and giver of all, then "all flesh will bless his holy name forever and ever" (v. 21).

For what need must you look to God today?
Where else have you been looking?

Thursday of the Third Week of Lent

READ EXODUS 16:4, 13–18

"I am going to rain bread from heaven for you."
—Exodus 16:4

Listen. 

Here we read the account of God feeding the people of Israel as they made their way through the wilderness, freed from their slavery in Egypt, but not having yet arrived in the land of promise. God's provision of bread for their journey is a familiar story. Every day, until the people came to Canaan and ate the fruit of their promised inheritance (Exod. 16:35; Josh. 5:12), they gathered a day's portion of this mysterious food that lay on the ground. The writer of Exodus tells us that the daily portion collected was sufficient to meet each person's need—there was nothing left over and there was no lack (Exod. 16:18). In this way, the Hebrew people were sustained by God with "bread from heaven." No matter what their condition, even through the days of their most faithless fears, when they forgot God's promises and complained (or even acted) against him, the manna lay on the ground in the morning. Manna became the daily reminder of God's presence with his people and of his unconditional love for them.

"Give us this day our daily bread," Jesus taught us to pray (Matt. 6:11, RSV). Like our forebears, we are making our own journey, in complete dependence each day upon the One who is completely dependable. The "manna" he gives, in whatever form, is evidence of an unconditional love that once took on human flesh and dwelt among us. *For the bread of God is that which comes down from heaven and gives life to the world* (John 6:33).

What sign do you have today of God's unconditional love for you?
What "manna" can you gather as a reminder of his presence with you?

Friday of the Third Week of Lent

READ PHILIPPIANS 4:14–20

And my God will fully satisfy every need of yours according to his riches in glory in Christ Jesus.
—Philippians 4:19

Listen. 

Paul's letter to the Philippians is a good pairing with this week's antiphon. It has been called the "joyful epistle," in part because of Paul's exhortation to "rejoice in the Lord always" (Phil. 4:4), but also because the entire message of this letter rings with a tone of joy and thanksgiving. Nowhere is this more apparent than in these closing verses.

It's important to remember that Paul wrote this letter while in prison. Rather than squelching his gospel message, his imprisonment actually advanced it, giving Paul the opportunity to speak of Christ even to his captors (Phil. 1:12–14). Nevertheless, prison is still prison, and while in captivity Paul was dependent upon the generosity of others to help and sustain him. Apparently, the church in Philippi generously rose to the occasion and sent gifts to Paul via an envoy named Epaphroditus. As he concludes his letter, Paul's joy and gratitude for their kindness is palpable. He sees in their gifts to him the providential hand of God, and Paul is confident that that same hand will always provide for them as well. This is no empty platitude; his own experience assures him of this.

"Riches in glory" is what Paul calls the heavenly storehouse from which God supplies the needs of his people. The Complete Jewish Bible defines it as God's "glorious wealth." The point is that

God's generosity knows no bounds—he who did not withhold his own Son from us, "will he not with him also give us everything else?" (Rom. 8:32).

What "gift" have you recently received that has blessed or enriched you?
Can you see the hand of God behind the giver?
"Rejoice in the Lord" for it today.

Saturday of the Third Week of Lent

Read Acts 27:33–38

After [Paul] had said this, he took bread,
and giving thanks to God in the presence of all,
he broke it and began to eat.
—Acts 27:35

Listen. 

A last supper on a raging sea. A simple meal of bread to make weary bodies and fearful souls ready for the fight of their lives. Shipwreck was inescapable, and death seemed all but certain . . . but Paul made everyone eat breakfast.

You have to read Acts 27 in its entirety to get the significance of what Paul did on that fateful morning. He was on his way to Rome for the purpose of giving witness to Christ. Yes, he was a prisoner of the Roman Empire, but even more, a prisoner of Christ (Eph. 4:1) and bound to God's purposes. His quiet confidence in the storm ran completely counter to the franticness of his shipmates. The God who held him fast had promised Paul that no life would be lost (v. 23–24). Based upon that promise, Paul took bread, gave thanks, and began to eat. These words allude closely to what Jesus did, don't they? Recall again the message of this week's antiphon: Jesus took bread, gave thanks, and the people ate their fill. Luke says that Paul and his companions finished their meal when all "had satisfied their hunger" (v. 38). Then they were ready.

Lent most definitely carries the message of our frailty and failure. Our mortality. "You are dust, and to dust you shall return" (Gen. 3:19). This is the shipwreck from which none of us can escape.

But Lent also affirms that our destiny goes beyond the shipwreck, and that God will faithfully give what is needed to make us ready.

Today, what promise from God do you need to trust in?

Sunday of the Fourth Week of Lent

ét-i- am si mórtu-us fú- e-rit, vi-vet : et omnis qui vi-vit

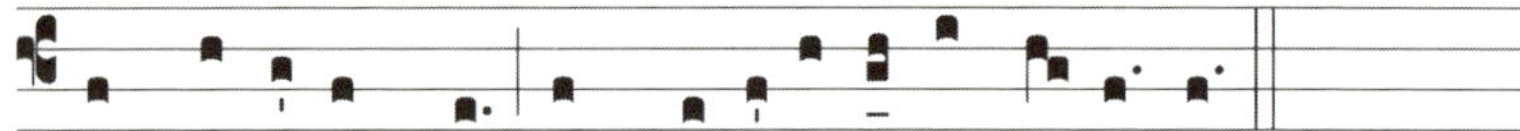

et cre-dit in me, non mo-ri- é-tur in ae-térnum.

Scan to Listen to
"Ego sum"

Ego sum resurrectio

ENGLISH TRANSLATION:

I am the resurrection and the life;
he who believes in me,
even if he dies, shall live;
and all who live and believe in me, shall never die.

Sunday of the Fourth Week of Lent

READ JOHN 11:1–27

"I am the resurrection and the life.
Those who believe in me, even though they die, will live,
and everyone who lives and believes in me will never die."
—John 11:25–26

John 11 records a pivotal event in Jesus's life—not to mention Lazarus's—and it is the context for the words of this week's antiphon, *Ego sum resurrectio.* The antiphon is taken from the Office of the Dead, a prayer cycle that honors the soul of a deceased person. As you listen to it through the week, recall this story of Lazarus and what it tells us about death, and life . . . and love.

The story begins with the news of Lazarus's illness reaching Jesus. The NRSVue translates it this way: "Accordingly, though Jesus loved Martha and her sister and Lazarus, after having heard that Lazarus was ill, he stayed two days longer in the place where he was" (v. 5–6). Jesus loved them, and *accordingly*, he stayed where he was. Jesus did not go immediately to Bethany, where he could have easily healed his friend Lazarus. Instead, he stayed put and, during that "delay," Lazarus died. Who can blame the grieving Martha for her almost accusative greeting to Jesus when he finally shows up: "Lord, if you had been here, my brother would not have died" (v. 21)? But, if Lazarus had not died, Martha, Mary, Lazarus, the disciples, and all the people of Bethany would never have been witnesses to one of the greatest truths of the gospel.

Martha looked to Jesus and hoped for a miracle of healing. Jesus looked to Martha and granted her a miracle beyond what she could imagine. It was Love who said to her, "I am the resurrection."

After Jesus declared to Martha, "I am the resurrection," he asked, "Do you believe this?" Do you*? And, if you do believe this, what difference does it make for your life?*

Monday of the Fourth Week of Lent

READ JOHN 3:1–17

For God so loved the world that he gave his only Son,
so that everyone who believes in him may not perish
but may have eternal life.
—John 3:16

Listen. 

Nicodemus had questions. We can assume that he had already heard Jesus teaching and perhaps he'd even witnessed a miracle or two. In any case, his interest was piqued and he looked for an opportunity to speak with Jesus face-to-face. That opportunity came at night when, as a Pharisee, Nicodemus could safely visit Jesus without attracting attention. And out of that night came one of the greatest statements of the entire New Testament. A summary of the gospel, really.

God *loved*, so he *gave*. It is the nature of love to give itself to another, to prefer the needs of the other above one's own, even to sacrifice for the sake of the other. "No one has greater love than this," said Jesus to his disciples, "to lay down one's life for one's friends" (John 15:13). We know at least two things from this gift: We are embraced by a love that is unconditional; and, as bearers of God's image, we are designed for *loving* and therefore *giving*.

John tells us that Nicodemus, giving expensive oils and spices, was among those who prepared the crucified Christ for burial (John 19:39). What did he believe about Jesus as he was anointing his body? Could this still be "the resurrection and the life" lying dead before him? Curiosity is what first led Nicodemus to Jesus. But it was far more than curiosity on that fateful night that compelled him to risk his profession, his reputation, and perhaps even his life.

What do you believe about God's love for you?

Tuesday of the Fourth Week of Lent

Read Romans 6:3–11

For if we have been united with him in a death like his,
we will certainly be united with him in a resurrection like his.
—Romans 6:5

Listen 

In many churches, Lent is a season of preparation for those who will be baptized at Easter. Whether viewed as a sacrament or as a symbol, baptism, according to Paul's letter to the Romans, inserts us into the life of Christ. Paul says we were "united with him," so that, in some mysterious way, Jesus took us with him to the cross, to the grave, and to his resurrection. Baptism, says Paul, is like our being buried and raised up again with Christ, an outward sign of our death to an old way of life and our birth into something entirely new. Just as Jesus rose from the grave, our coming up from the waters of baptism represents our own resurrection into a life that is no longer dominated by sin and death. These enemies have been dethroned by what Jesus accomplished on the cross and in the grave. Jesus Christ alone is Lord and, as one baptismal prayer puts it, "We have been marked and sealed as his own, forever."

The understanding and practice of baptism has varied in the church (and sometimes divided it) for centuries. It is enough for us to believe what Martha was invited to believe—that Jesus is the resurrection and the life. Even if we are not preparing for baptism at Easter, we can remember through Lent that Jesus has introduced himself to us in the same way, and so invited us to share in all the benefits of his own dying and rising again.

Say a prayer today for new believers around the world who are preparing for their baptism at Easter. These are our brothers and sisters "in Christ."

Wednesday of the Fourth Week of Lent

READ 1 CORINTHIANS 15:1–22

For since death came through a human,
the resurrection of the dead has also come through a human,
for as all die in Adam, so all will be made alive in Christ.
—1 Corinthians 15:21–22

Listen. 

We cannot talk about Christ's rising without also talking about our falling, for the one is God's supreme and final answer to the other. "In the day you eat of it," warned God about the forbidden fruit in the garden, "you shall die" (Gen. 2:17). What follows, we know, is an account of Adam and Eve's defiance, and of the terrible consequences of their choices.

God made good on his promise to our first parents, in a "curse" that contains those awful words that haunt us every Ash Wednesday: "By the sweat of your face you shall eat bread until you return to the ground, for out of it you were taken; *you are dust, and to dust you shall return*" (3:19, emphasis added). Lent reminds us that we are all participants in the tragic events of Genesis 3, every bit as much as if you and I were Adam and Eve. (Can any of us honestly believe that we would have done any better than they?) We all bear the wonder of God's image, crafted by his hand and in his likeness (Gen. 1:26). We also bear the proof of the image's brokenness, a proof that is no more dreadfully evident than in death.

But, if we believe the gospel, then we know that God already had in mind the means by which he would repair us. Our dying "in Adam," as Paul puts it, is answered, supremely and finally, by our being made alive "in Christ." *Ego sum resurrectio*—Christ is our resurrection hope.

What difference would it make if you did not *believe in the resurrection?*

Thursday of the Fourth Week of Lent

READ PSALM 16

For you do not give me up to Sheol or let your faithful one see the Pit. You show me the path of life. In your presence there is fullness of joy; in your right hand are pleasures forevermore.

—Psalm 16:10–11

Listen. 

On the day of Pentecost, Peter stood before the crowd gathered in Jerusalem for the festival. They had witnessed something extraordinary happening to Jesus's followers—the Holy Spirit filling them—and Peter wanted to explain what they had seen and heard (see Acts 2:1–21). After reminding everyone of God's promise of the Spirit, he spoke about Jesus, about his life, death, and resurrection. Wanting to describe for them that Jesus's rising from the dead was also the fulfillment of God's promise, Peter quoted from Psalm 16 (see Acts 2:24–36). It was the first time the book of Psalms was used by the church to explain who Christ was and what he had done.

Jesus himself had singled out the Psalms as especially revelatory when he met with his disciples after his resurrection. He explained that everything he'd taught them was to disclose God's purposes, "that everything written about me in the law of Moses, the prophets, *and the psalms* must be fulfilled" (Lk. 24:44, emphasis added). It is no wonder that the book of Psalms soon became the official, daily "prayer book" of the church. (St. Benedict wanted all the psalms prayed each week. The early desert monks recited all 150 each day!) Not a second goes by without the voice of the psalms being sounded somewhere in the world.

So, it seems especially pertinent to recall during Lent that the church's first public use of the psalms was to explain the Lord's resurrection. Luke tells us (Acts 2:41) that 3,000 people were baptized as a result!

What is your favorite psalm? Imagine it as the words of *Jesus, or words* about *Jesus, or words* to *Jesus. What is this psalm telling you?*

Friday of the Fourth Week of Lent

Read Isaiah 26:16–19

Your dead shall live; their corpses shall rise.
Those who dwell in the dust will awake and shout for joy!
For your dew is a radiant dew,
and the earth will give birth to those long dead.
—Isaiah 26:19

Listen. 

This week's antiphon carries the central message of the gospel in the words of Jesus—*I am the resurrection and the life*—and every book of the New Testament revolves around this blazing truth. But, like the verses from Psalm 16 that we read yesterday, the Old Testament prophets also spoke of the promise of a resurrected life.

On one level, we can hear the words of Isaiah as a promise to a nation which, in the face of impending destruction, can count on the power of God to raise it up from the dust once again. The imagery is dramatic, even disturbing. In its present and seemingly hopeless condition, the nation is like a woman crying in her birth pangs, but her cries are as fruitless as her womb (v. 18). There is no life to be born, and she is inconsolable. But, declares the prophet, "your dead *shall* live." The dew of heaven shall renew the ground, and the dust itself shall yield up its fallen inhabitants. Something shall be done that God alone can do, and hopeless mourning shall be turned to songs of joy!

We know the prophet is pointing to something more than the rebirth of one nation; he says so one chapter before (see Isa. 25:6–9):

“[The Lord] will destroy on this mountain the shroud that is cast over all peoples, the covering that is spread over all nations; he will swallow up death forever.” Then, says Isaiah, “the Lord God will wipe away the tears from all faces.”

Reflect on the story of Lazarus (John 11) in light of these words from Isaiah. What connections can you make?

Saturday of the Fourth Week of Lent

READ ROMANS 8:9–11, 22–25

If the Spirit of him who raised Jesus from the dead dwells in you,
he who raised Christ Jesus from the dead will give life to your mortal bodies
also through his Spirit that dwells in you.
—Romans 8:11

Listen 

When Jesus identified himself to Martha as "the resurrection and the life," he was doing more than preparing her for the raising of her brother. As miraculous as that was, there was so much more going on than this one-time event. Jesus was opening the curtain to an entirely new world of hope and possibility, a vista that could only be seen with the eyes of faith and hope. "Do you believe this?" Jesus asked her. With her heart grieving and her eyes filled with tears, Martha was being asked if she could nevertheless "see" Jesus for who he truly was. "Yes, Lord," she answered.

The same Spirit who raised Jesus—the divine Breath of God that refilled the lungs of his dead body—that same Spirit dwells in us, his followers. Paul is adamant about this. Yes, he acknowledges, we live an earthly life of mortality and sin, where flesh dies and the body decays. But, since the resurrection of Christ, we know that we were meant to breathe a more rarified air, and that, someday, we will. The Holy Spirit who lives in us now is God's guarantee.

It was C. S. Lewis who wrote, "Aim at heaven and you will get earth 'thrown in': aim at earth and you will get neither."

When you listen to the antiphon today, remember what Paul said about our waiting with all of creation for what we cannot yet see, and with eyes of faith and hope wide open, keep your aim toward heaven.

What does the hope of heaven mean to you?

Sunday of the Fifth Week of Lent

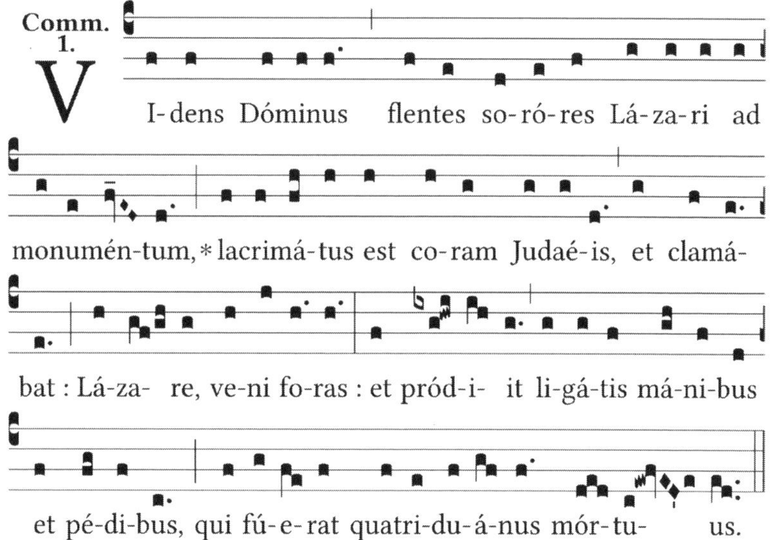

Scan to Listen to
"Videns Dominus"

Videns Dominus

English translation:

The Lord, seeing the sisters of Lazarus weeping at the tomb,
wept in the presence of the Jews,
and cried out: Lazarus, come forth.
And he who had been dead for four days came forth,
bound hands and feet.

Sunday of the Fifth Week of Lent

READ JOHN 11:33

When Jesus saw her weeping
and the Jews who came with her also weeping,
he was greatly disturbed in spirit and deeply moved.
—John 11:33

This week's antiphon (taken from the Communion rite for the fifth Sunday of Lent) connects phrases from five different verses of John chapter 11 to summarize the account of Jesus raising Lazarus from the grave. Last week, the story was introduced through Jesus's words to Martha, "I am the resurrection." This week, we explore significant details of what happened next.

Videns Dominus—"The Lord, seeing" (v. 33). We should not move too quickly through these opening words. Their significance may even be indicated by the music of the antiphon—notice how all five syllables are presented on the same pitch. "Pay special attention," it could be saying. There is something deeply reassuring about this brief phrase, isn't there? Who of us has not felt, from time to time, that God was not paying attention to what was happening to us? *Where are you, Lord?* we wonder. *Do you see what is going on?*

"And God saw the people of Israel, and God knew their condition" (Exod. 2:25, RSV). The deliverance of the Israelites is the premier story of God's saving love and power for his chosen people and a foreshadowing of what he would do through his only Son. It is the Easter of the Old Testament. Among other things, it tells us that God was never ignorant of his people's sufferings. God *saw*. And then, he did something about it.

Videns Dominus—Jesus *saw* the inconsolable grief of Lazarus's family and friends. He knew their condition. And then, he did something about it.

Listen to the antiphon again and pay special attention to the opening. What more do you hear?

Monday of the Fifth Week of Lent

READ JOHN 11:35

Jesus began to weep.
—John 11:35

Listen. 

Following John's record of events, this week's antiphon tells us what took place when Jesus saw Lazarus's family and friends mourning their loved one's untimely death. Grief seems to have engulfed the entire village, but before doing anything *about* it, Jesus first immersed himself *in* it.

"Jesus began to weep." Let it never be thought that the Son of man does not sympathize with us in our pain. Those who were with Mary and Martha that sorrowful day saw and heard the truth of the incarnation in a profound way. Divine compassion cried with human tears. Like those he came to save, Jesus too was "a man of sorrows, and acquainted with grief" (Isa. 53:3, RSV). What other than Jesus's full and most vulnerable humanity can explain the grief he felt when he saw Mary weeping at the loss of her brother? What other than his unbounded sympathy can explain the tears he shed?

Psalm 56 uses a wonderfully mysterious image to express God's sympathy for us in our times of sorrow: "You have kept count of my tossings; put my tears in your bottle. Are they not in your record?" (v. 8). The psalmist imagines God keeping meticulous record of our sufferings. Not only does he log every pain, but he also stores every tear in a bottle. Like each sparrow that drops from the sky, each tear we shed is known to God (Matt. 10:29) and, according to the psalmist, kept by him. Thus was the sympathy of heaven witnessed that day in Bethany, when Jesus wept.

Imagine Jesus standing with you in your own grief. What is he doing?

Tuesday of the Fifth Week of Lent

READ JOHN 11:38–39

Jesus said, "Take away the stone."
—John 11:39

Listen. 

John 11:39 is not a verse included in this week's antiphon. But for the sake of understanding what happens next in the story—and in the antiphon—we must consider it.

We've seen that Jesus is moved to tears when he sees the sorrow of his friends. But he comes to do so much more than bring comfort to the grieving. He comes to bring life to the dead. At this point in his ministry, Jesus has raised two people from the dead—a widow's son and a synagogue official's daughter (Lk. 7:11–17; 8:40–56). What was remarkable about Lazarus, however, is that his body had been dead for four days, bound in funeral cloths, and buried in a tomb!

Martha's objection to removing the stone was practical—Lazarus's body would have already suffered decay and there would be an awful smell (the Bible is nothing if not blunt). In what was about to take place, Martha would know that Jesus was not speaking symbolically when he said, "I am the resurrection and the life." Lazarus walked out with a body that was whole and well, in every detail. Jesus is Lord over death *and* decay, and both yield up their captives at his command.

One other thought. When Jesus cried, "Take away the stone," is it possible that the thought of another tomb and another stone crossed his mind? Did he picture a dark grave? Did he hear another voice commanding, *Take away the stone*? (see Matt. 28:2).

Is there a "stone" standing between you and the fullness of life that Jesus intends for you? If so, what is it?

Wednesday of the Fifth Week of Lent

Read John 11:40–43

He cried with a loud voice, "Lazarus, come out!"
—John 11:43

Listen. 

The creation account in Genesis tells us that God began to bring order out of formless emptiness when he spoke, "Let there be light," and there was light (Gen. 1:3). In the beginning, the voice of God spoke the will of God, and what did not yet exist was brought into being. "The voice of the Lord is powerful," sang the psalmist, "the voice of the Lord is full of majesty" (Ps. 29:4). Perhaps even that is an understatement, for how does one describe a voice that will be obeyed even when there is nothing yet in existence to obey it?

It comes as no surprise, then, that we hear an echo of this voice in the words of Jesus. For example, when Jesus once commanded the stormy sea: "Peace! Be still!" immediately there came a great calm. His relieved disciples were in awe, and they wondered who this could be "that even the wind and the sea obey him" (Mk. 4:39–41). And there was the Roman soldier who believed in the power of Jesus's word when he declined Jesus's offer to come to his home: "Lord, . . . just say the word, and my servant will be healed" (Matt. 8:8, NIV).

This week's antiphon reminds us that, as much as he sympathizes with our sorrows, Jesus does much more. A shoulder to cry on is what we all want. But, eventually, a voice that will raise the dead is what we all need. "Lazarus, come out," was spoken by that voice. Is there any doubt, then, about what would happen next?

In what situation in your life do you need to hear the voice of Jesus?

Thursday of the Fifth Week of Lent

READ JOHN 11:44

The dead man came out, his hands and feet bound with strips of cloth and his face wrapped in a cloth. Jesus said to them, "Unbind him, and let him go."

—John 11:44

Listen. 

"The dead man came out." A man who had been dead for four days, whose body had begun to decay and, according to Jewish teaching, whose soul would have already departed—this man was now standing before what must have been a gawking crowd of witnesses. (One can only imagine what Lazarus himself must have been feeling!) This week's antiphon leaves us with an image of the risen Lazarus, presenting himself before Jesus, with hands and feet still bound by his burial cloths. John says that his face was still covered as well. So, Jesus had one further instruction to give.

"Unbind him, and let him go." At the very start of his public ministry, Jesus quoted from the prophet Isaiah to describe his commission from God: "He has sent me to proclaim release to the captives . . . to set free those who are oppressed" (Lk. 4:18). When Jesus told the people to unbind the resurrected Lazarus, he gave us a poignant illustration of this good news. Aren't these words what we all want to hear? To be let loose from whatever strips of death have already managed to wind themselves around us? Regret blinds our eyes from envisioning future dreams; guilt straps down our shoulders and ties up our arms, restricting our embrace of life, or of others; and fear clutches so at our ankles that we walk in God's ways with a shuffle instead of running with the wind. "Unbind him, and let him go."

What strip of grave cloth has wrapped itself around your heart?
What is Jesus saying to you about being unbound?

Friday of the Fifth Week of Lent

Read Isaiah 25:6–8

He will swallow up death forever.
Then the Lord God will wipe away the tears from all faces,
and the disgrace of his people he will take away from all the earth,
for the Lord has spoken.
—Isaiah 25:8

Listen. 

The importance of Lazarus's story cannot be overstated. This is why we have spent several days exploring it—with two antiphons drawn from it as John records it in his Gospel and through the lens of various Scripture passages. Raising Lazarus is the climax of Jesus's public ministry and the prelude to his own rising. From this point, John's Gospel begins to unfold the events of Christ's passion—his own death and resurrection.

Today's passage from the prophet Isaiah speaks of a future feast of celebration that will be for "all peoples." The feast will be held because the last and common enemy of all the nations of the earth will be destroyed (see 1 Cor. 15:26). Death is pictured as a dark shroud that overshadows everyone, a pall that covers the whole world. But death's end will be its own death. It will be swallowed up—ingested and consumed, as it were—by God himself. And to mark the occasion, God will spread an abundant table and host a joyful festival, to which everyone is invited.

It doesn't require the season of Lent to make us mindful of our mortality. All pain is a kind of harbinger of death. But resurrection life has its couriers, too. Isaiah's words are among them, as is the story of Lazarus. Even more, if we follow the Gospel of John to its conclusion, we know the final Victor, and his invitation to God's banquet is the golden ticket. Because of Christ, wrote the apostle Paul, "Death has been swallowed up in victory" (1 Cor. 15:54).

What message does Christ's victory over death bring to the pain you may be suffering today?

Saturday of the Fifth Week of Lent

READ PSALM 30

Weeping may linger for the night, but joy comes with the morning.
—Psalm 30:5

Listen. 

We are approaching the "night" of Jesus's suffering and death. As he said to those who came to arrest him in the Garden of Gethsemane, "This is your hour, and the power of darkness!" (Lk. 22:53). Or, after Judas left the upper room to betray Jesus, John makes the weighted point, "And it was night" (John 13:30). In every way imaginable, Jesus would soon be engulfed in the darkness of the night.

But, as we leave the story of Lazarus, we are reminded that nights pass and mornings come. While Jesus wept with the grief of his friends, within only a few short minutes, he gave them an overwhelming reason for rejoicing. Their darkness (and certainly Lazarus's) was turned to light when Jesus called out, "Lazarus, come out."

Psalm 30 is a song of thanksgiving to God for an act of divine deliverance that the psalmist likens to being brought up from Sheol and restored back into the morning light. Is it too much to imagine that the next time Lazarus heard this psalm in the synagogue, he could have thought that it was written for him? These are words we cling to as we approach Holy Week, and certainly as we experience our own "nights." Jesus must have done so. The writer to the Hebrews says that "for the sake of the joy that was set before him [Jesus] endured the cross" (12:2). If even the Son of God looked forward to the coming dawn, shouldn't we as well?

What part of your life feels like "night"?
How can you express to God your hope for "morning"?

Palm Sunday: Sunday of the Passion

Scan to Listen to
"Hosanna"

Hosanna

English translation:

Hosanna to the son of David.
Blessed is he who comes in the name of the Lord.
He is the King of Israel:
Hosanna in the highest.

Palm Sunday: Sunday of the Passion

READ MATTHEW 21:1–11

"Hosanna to the Son of David! Blessed is the one who comes in the name of the Lord! Hosanna in the highest heaven!"
—Matthew 21:9

Today's antiphon—the traditional procession antiphon for Palm Sunday—sounds a clear tone of triumph and solemnity. The flowing and uplifting movement of the chant itself expresses the mood of celebration, and the text, taken directly from the Gospel accounts, is a greeting filled with joy and hope (see also Ps. 118:19–26, from which this text is taken). It is addressed to the Son of David, heir to the throne, the King of Israel.

But, what kind of king is this? As he makes his way into the city, he is cheered by the crowd and, as would have been done for Israel's kings of old, his path is spontaneously paved with palms, branches, and even clothing. But he is neither standing in a chariot nor mounted upon a warrior steed. He is riding on a donkey, a humble beast of burden. Anyone who knew the Scriptures, knew that this was a fulfillment of Zechariah's prophetic oracle: *See, your king comes to you; triumphant and victorious is he, humble and riding on a donkey, on a colt, the foal of a donkey* (Zech. 9:9). He is King, yes, but of what kingdom?

Palm Sunday processions are taking place all across the world today, including Jerusalem. Palm branches are being waved in commemoration of the Triumphal Entry, and in many cases this antiphon is being sung. And everywhere, in some way or another, this acclamation is being made: *Hosanna—God save!* What kind of King is hailed with such words?

Spend a few moments today envisioning yourself in the crowd in Jerusalem that day. What is it you are hoping for?

Monday of Holy Week

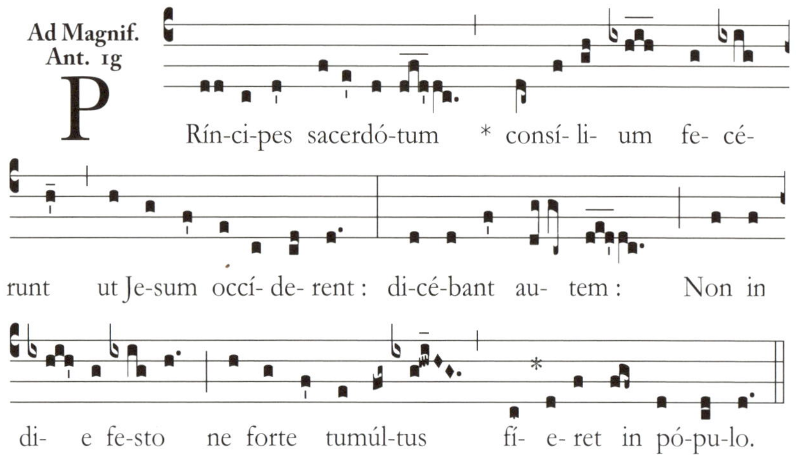

Scan to Listen to
"Principes sacerdotum"

Principes sacerdotum

English translation:

The chief priests took counsel that they might kill Jesus;
but they said: Not on the festival day,
lest there should be a tumult among the people.

Monday of Holy Week

READ JOHN 11:45–50

[The high priest said:] "You do not understand that it is better for you to have one man die for the people than to have the whole nation destroyed."
—John 11:50

Last week we left the story of Lazarus with the picture of Jesus's newly risen friend standing alive at the mouth of his own tomb. Two things happened in that moment: First, Jesus's power as the Son of God was seen by all and welcomed by his followers; second, events were set into motion that would eventually lead to Jesus's death. From that moment on, it was determined by some that the Giver of life would need to have his own life taken away.

With cold brevity, today's antiphon sums up what John and Matthew record about the authorities' decision to arrest and kill Jesus (also see Matt. 26:3–5). News of what Jesus had done in Bethany had reached their itching ears, and they could not imagine such power being anything other than a threat both to themselves and to the status quo that they worked so hard to protect. The religious leaders rationalized their ugly assessment of things by dressing it in a robe of security and concern for the welfare of the people in their "care."

Put together, yesterday's and today's antiphons are evidence of the astonishing speed with which Holy Week moves us from a triumphant welcome to a brutal denouncement. In turns out, however, that these worldly judges were unknowingly arguing for heaven's point of view. For entirely the wrong reasons they were coming to the right conclusion—Jesus needed to die for the sake of others.

What does Caiaphas's pronouncement tell you about God's ways and purposes?

Tuesday of Holy Week

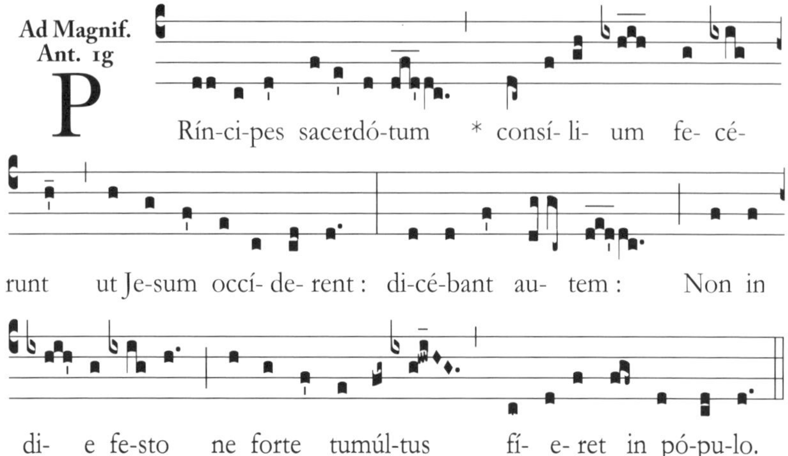

Scan to Listen to
"Principes sacerdotum"

Principes sacerdotum

English translation:

The chief priests took counsel that they might kill Jesus;
but they said: Not on the festival day,
lest there should be a tumult among the people.

Tuesday of Holy Week

Read John 11:51–53

[The high priest] prophesied that Jesus was about to die for the nation,
and not for the nation only,
but to gather into one the dispersed children of God.
—John 11:51–52

"The chief priests made a plan to kill Jesus," says the antiphon. Caiaphas had it right, of course. Jesus needed to die. Caiaphas's office as "high priest that year" put him into the position to speak with authority, even prophetically, as John puts it (v. 51). Later, as if to emphasize the point, when John describes the night of Jesus's betrayal, trial, and beating, he identifies Caiaphas once again as the one who had advocated for Jesus's death for the sake of all the people (John 18:14).

We must see again, during these dramatic days of Holy Week, that while plans were being drawn up by Caiaphas, the chief priests, and their council, God's plan was already firmly in place and had been since "before the foundation of the world" (1 Pet. 1:19–20). The wisdom of the Book of Proverbs puts it this way: "The human mind may devise many plans, but it is the purpose of the Lord that will be established" (19:21).

During these coming days of Holy Week, not a single moment passed in the life of Jesus outside the sovereign will of God—nor outside the shelter of his love. Yes, love. Love was clearly not what compelled Caiaphas and his committee to devise their scheme for Jesus's death. But love had always (and here, *always* means *eternally*) been the real power behind God's scheme, and his Son's human life. "I am the good shepherd," Jesus said. "The good shepherd lays down his life for the sheep" (John 10:11). God's purpose and God's love are inseparable.

What is taking place in your life right now where you need to see the love of God at work?

Wednesday of Holy Week

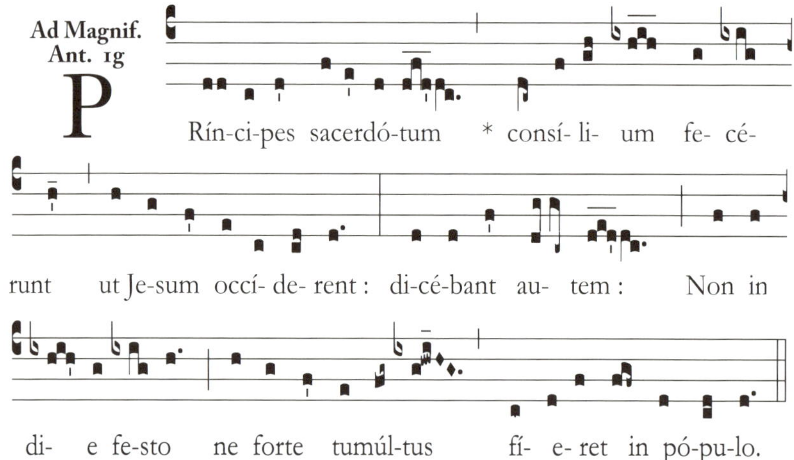

Scan to Listen to
"Principes sacerdotum"

Principes sacerdotum

English translation:

The chief priests took counsel that they might kill Jesus;
but they said: Not on the festival day,
lest there should be a tumult among the people.

Wednesday of Holy Week

Read Psalm 2:1–4a

Why do the nations conspire and the peoples plot in vain?
—Psalm 2:1

One of the earliest recorded prayers of the church appears in Acts 4. Peter and John, who'd been imprisoned for "proclaiming that in Jesus there is the resurrection of the dead" (v. 2), were released under threat of punishment if they did not cease their preaching. The two apostles found their friends, and rather than running away in fear, they raised their voices in prayer, quoting from the opening two verses of Psalm 2. When they finished their prayers, the Acts record that the whole place shook, the Holy Spirit filled everyone who was there, and they all went back out to speak the word of God "with boldness" (see Acts 4:23–31).

Why *do* the rulers take counsel together against the Lord, and against his Anointed? As we read these words and listen to the antiphon for the last time this week, we recall that the plotting of Jesus's enemies really was in vain—first, because heaven was overseeing a plan that so far surpassed the schemes of any human authority that nothing on earth could alter it; second, because they utterly failed in their efforts to avoid "an uproar among the people." The uproar that concerned them was an uprising by Jesus's supporters that would eventually bring down the wrath of Rome. In this regard, they could be satisfied with their efforts. But, what they did not and could not foresee was that, following the successful completion of their plans, an uproar of such magnitude ensued that the whole world was turned upside down (Acts 17:6).

Take a few minutes today to pray in preparation for "walking with Jesus" through the events of the coming days.

Holy Thursday

℣. Ne nos mente di-vi-dá-mur cave-ámus.

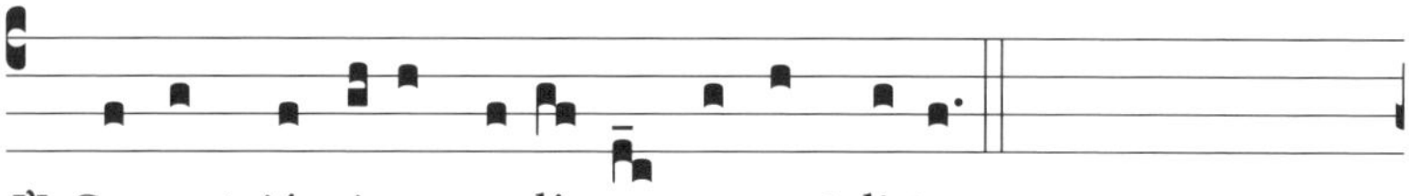

℣. Cessent iúrgi- a ma-lígna, cessent li-tes.

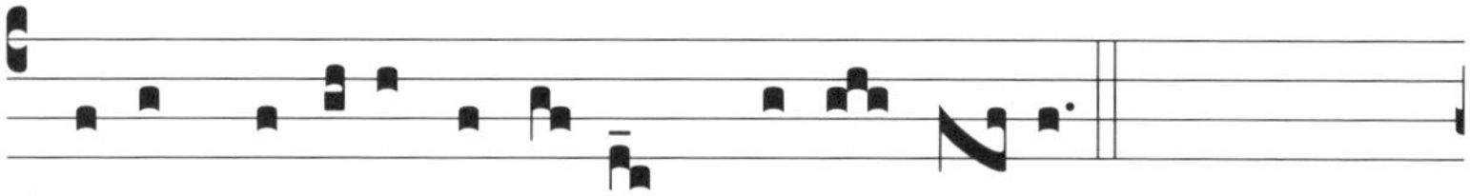

℣. Et in mé-di- o nostri sit Christus De- us.

Ant. Ubi cá-ri-tas est ve-ra, De-us i-bi est.

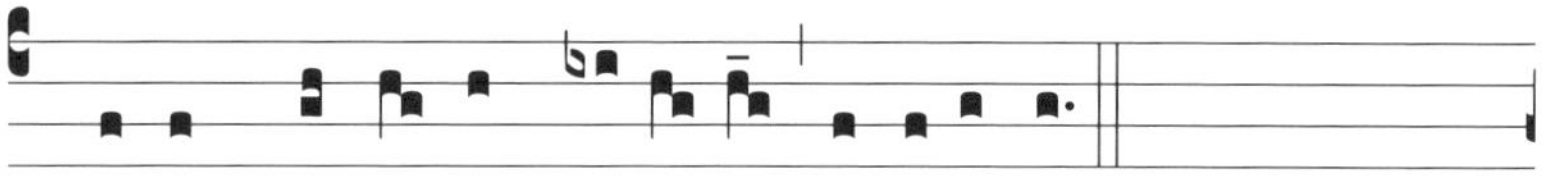

℣. Simul quoque cum be- á- tis vi-de-ámus.

℣. Glo-ri- ánter vul-tum tu- um, Christe De-us:

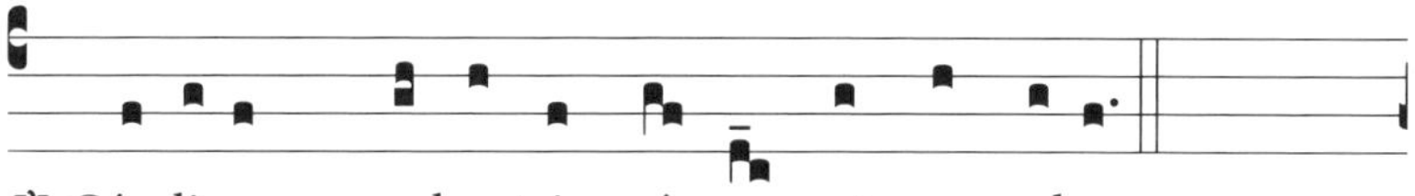

℣. Gáudi- um, quod est imménsum, atque probum.

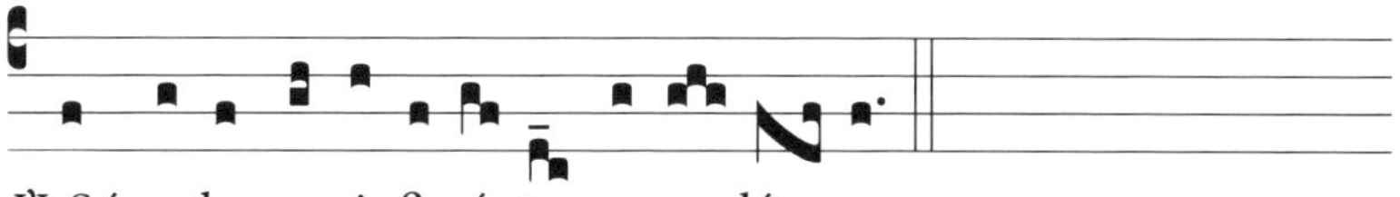

℣. Sǽcu-la per infi-ní- ta sæcu- ló- rum.

Scan to Listen to
"Ubi caritas"

Holy Thursday

Ubi caritas

English translation:

Antiphon: *Where there is charity and love, God is there.*

℣. *The love of Christ has gathered us into one.*
Let us exult and rejoice in this.
Let us fear and love the living God.
And from a sincere heart, let us love one another.

℣. *Therefore, when we gather as one,*
Let us beware that we are not divided in mind.
Let malicious quarrels end; let contentions cease.
And may Christ our God be in the midst of us.

℣. *And in company with the blessed*
May we see your face, in glory,
Pure and unbounded joy,
For ages without end. Amen.

Holy Thursday

READ JOHN 13:34–35

I give you a new commandment, that you love one another. Just as I have loved you, you also should love one another.
—John 13:34

"Where love is, there is God." *Ubi caritas* is a hymn that dates to the earliest centuries of the church. It especially has come to be associated with the liturgical rites of Holy Thursday, with the celebration of the Lord's Supper, and, in particular, with the foot washing.

On this night, Jesus washed the feet of his disciples, and in doing so he gave them an example of how they should live with one another and love one another (John 13:1–15). John records that Jesus rose from the table and exchanged the outer robe he was wearing for a simple towel wrapped around his waist. Then he knelt before each of his followers and, as would a common servant, he washed their feet, using the towel with which he was clothed to dry them. Imagining the scene is arresting enough. Actually experiencing it must have been, in a very literal sense, too wonderful for words.

"Love one another just as I have loved you," Jesus commanded them. What he had just done at the table and what he was soon to do at the cross—laying down his life for his friends—was nothing less than the love of God in the flesh. The disciples were to be carriers of that same love. "The love of Christ has gathered us into one," says the hymn. So, "from a sincere heart, let us love another."

When the meal was over, Jesus went with his disciples to a garden at the foot of the Mount of Olives, called Gethsemane. Love stayed on its course.

Listen again to "Ubi caritas."
How does it help you understand your own calling as a follower of Jesus?

Good Friday

Grad. 5.

CHri-stus * factus est pro no- bis obé-

di- ens us-que ad mor-tem, mor-tem au-tem

cru- cis. ℣. Propter quod et De-us exal-

tá-vit illum, et de-

dit il-li no- men, quod est super omne

no- men.

Scan to Listen to "Christus factus"

English translation:

Christ became obedient for us unto death,
even to death upon a cross.

℣. *Therefore God has highly exalted him,*
and given him the name that is above every name.

Good Friday

Read Philippians 2:5–11

He humbled himself and became obedient to the point of death, even death on a cross. Therefore God exalted him even more highly and gave him the name that is above every other name.
—Philippians 2:8–9

Today's chant piece, *Christus factus est*, is taken from Paul's Letter to the Philippians. Read within its fuller context, it is part of Paul's exhortation for humility and unity in the body of Christ. It has been argued by some that he may be quoting directly, or at least drawing words from, a hymn that was already being used in the nascent church, making the singing of these verses one of the oldest liturgical practices of Christianity. Whatever their origins, these phrases are both poetic and compact, and they describe with profound clarity the mysteries of Christ's incarnation, crucifixion, resurrection, and glorification.

For this reason, *Christus factus est* has come to be most associated with the days of the Paschal Triduum—Holy Thursday through Holy Saturday. While it is sometimes used as a Gradual, a more traditional use has been to sing the first part, ending in "death," on Holy Thursday; to add the phrase "death on a cross" on Good Friday; and to chant the entire piece on Holy Saturday. Listening to the piece as a whole reminds us of the full account of what took place over these three sacred days.

Mortem autem crucis—"even death on a cross." It wasn't just that Jesus died for us, nor even that he was executed. It was that the means by which he willingly sacrificed himself was thoroughly cruel and, in his case, thoroughly unjust. On the day we call Good Friday, a wholly and purely innocent Victim was slain in a manner reserved for criminals. He was crucified.

Listen to how the chant presents the character and meaning of each word or phrase. What word or words particularly capture your attention?

Holy Saturday

Scan to Listen to
"Alleluia"

Alleluia

English translation:

Alleluia.
Give thanks to the Lord, for he is good;
because his mercy is forever.

Holy Saturday

Read Psalm 107:1–3

O give thanks to the Lord, for he is good,
for his steadfast love endures forever.
—Psalm 107:1

Something strange is happening. There is a great silence on earth today, a great silence and stillness. The whole earth keeps silence because the King is asleep." So begins an ancient homily for Holy Saturday—the day that Christ descended into hell, vanquished the devil, and flung wide the gates of death. "Lift up your heads, O gates! and be lifted up, O ancient doors, that the King of glory may come in!" It's easy to see why this verse from Psalm 24 is often sung on this day. Even in the stillness, there begins the sound of approaching Victory.

Thus the day begins. But it ends quite differently. At the Paschal Vigil, the nighttime liturgy that ushers in Easter morning, a word is proclaimed that, in many traditions, has itself been asleep and buried for more than forty days—*Alleluia!* In preparation for the reading from one of the Gospel accounts of the Resurrection (Matt. 28:1–10; Mk. 16:1–8; Lk. 24:1–9), a cantor, or choir leader, intones the *Alleluia*, and the congregation responds (in some places accompanied by ringing bells, and often repeated three times, with a rise in pitch each time). Then, the celebratory sound gives way to a full-throated song: "O give thanks to the Lord, for he is good!"

What, other than the goodness and mercy of God, could have brought us to this day? What, other than joy and thanksgiving, could be our fitting response?

As you look back through the days of Lent, what are you most grateful for? How can you bring that gratitude into your celebration of Easter?

Easter Sunday
The Resurrection of the Lord

Intr. 4.

RESURREXI, * et adhuc te-cum sum, al-

le- lú- ia: po- su- í-sti su- per me ma- num tu-

am, al- le- lú- ia: mi-rá- bi-lis fac- ta est sci-

én-ti- a tu- a, alle- lú-ia, al- le- lú- ia. *Ps.*

Dómi-ne probásti me, et cogno-vísti me: tu cogno-vísti

sessi- ónem me-am, et re-surrecti- ó-nem me-am.

Scan to Listen to
"Resurrexi"

Resurrexi

English translation:

I have risen, and I am still with you, alleluia;
you have put your hand on me, alleluia;
your knowledge has become wonderful, alleluia, alleluia.

℣. *Lord, you have searched me and known me,*
you have known my sitting down and my rising up again.

Easter Sunday
The Resurrection of the Lord

Read Luke 24:1–12

"He is not here but has risen."
—Luke 24:5

Today is Easter Sunday, the celebration of the resurrection of Jesus Christ. After a long season of Lent, and a solemn Holy Week of remembrance, all over the world today in hundreds of languages, people are exchanging greetings with one another with the joyful acclamation and response: "The Lord is risen! He is risen indeed!" (see Lk. 24:33–34). One might imagine that any worship service on this day would begin with loud shouts, the ringing of bells, and the exultant sound of trumpets and horns, and all of that would be more than appropriate for giving voice to our praises. But the chant piece we are listening to today begins with a different sound and a different voice.

The Introit that opens the liturgy of the Eucharist on Easter morning imagines a tomb in a garden near Jerusalem. Hidden from the view of all but heaven's eyes, Jesus the Christ—the crucified, dead, and buried Son of God—as if just awakened from sleep, lays aside his burial cloths, arises from his stone bed, and stands up. Then, before facing the world he has just saved, he faces the Father who sent him, and his first words are a prayer.

"I have risen, Father, and I am still with you. You placed your hand on me from my birth and it is still upon me. You have seen everything. You saw my falling down, and now you have seen my rising up. Your knowledge is too wonderful for words. Alleluia!"

Imagine you are the first to greet Jesus on Easter morning. What would you do? What would you say to him?

Monday of Easter Week

Monday of Easter Week

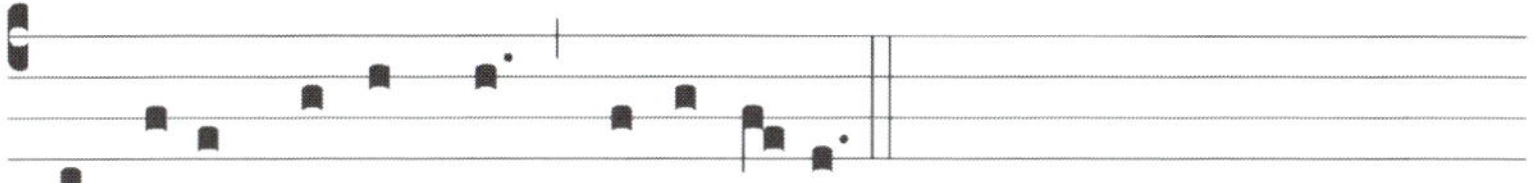

Scan to Listen to
"Victimae paschali"

Victimae paschali

English translation:

Let Christians offer praises To the paschal Victim.
The lamb has redeemed the sheep:
The Innocent Christ has reconciled
sinners to the Father.
Death and life battle In an amazing duel:
The dead Leader of Life
Reigns alive.
Tell us, Mary, What did you see on the way?
The sepulchre of the living Christ
And I saw the glory of the Risen One:
The angel witnesses, The head cloth and the clothing.
Christ my hope has risen:
He is preceding His own to Galilee.
We know the Christ has truly risen.
From the Dead:
Conquerer King,
Be merciful to us.

Monday of Easter Week

READ MATTHEW 28:1–10

"Then go quickly and tell his disciples,
'He has been raised from the dead,
and indeed he is going ahead of you to Galilee;
there you will see him.'"
—Matthew 28:7

The final piece of chant that we will hear is appointed for use on Easter Sunday and every day during Easter week. *Victimae paschali laudes* belongs to a collection of pieces known as "sequences." The name comes from a Latin word (*sequi*) which means "to follow." These were sung texts, hymns of a sort, that followed the "Alleluia" and led directly to the Gospel reading. Though in modern use they now come before the "Alleluia," their name nevertheless has been retained. *Victimae* is the only one designated to be used for an entire week; this says something about this sequence, and even more about these seven special days.

Yesterday, we imagined the mystery of Jesus's private interaction with the Father immediately following his resurrection. Today we turn to the bustle of public activity that quickly followed. All the Gospel accounts agree (and here we must remember that each Gospel writer focused on what took place from a particular angle) that Mary Magdalene was among the first to come to the empty tomb. Matthew records that she and her companions were greeted by a radiant angel who charged them to go and tell the disciples that Christ had risen from death . . . and that he wants to see them all.

Today, we do well to remember that, like the disciples, we too have heard the good news of Christ's resurrection from someone else—a friend, a parent, a pastor, a teacher, or perhaps one of the Gospel writers. Our faith was born of hearing (Rom. 10:14–15), and whoever it was who spoke was sent to tell us that Jesus is alive.

How did you first hear the good news of Jesus Christ? Take a moment to recall the ones who first "spoke" the Gospel to you, and give thanks to God for them.

Tuesday of Easter Week

READ 1 CORINTHIANS 5:7–8

For our paschal lamb, Christ, has been sacrificed.
Therefore, let us celebrate the festival. . . .
—1 Corinthians 5:7–8

"Let Christians offer praises to the Paschal Victim."

Listen.

Like so many medieval hymns of its kind (and not unlike the Bible itself), *Victimae paschali laudes* uses word play and paradox to express some of its central images: A lamb rescues the sheep, an innocent saves sinners, death and life do battle, a dead leader reigns immortal. This approach is used in the opening line, inviting all Christians to offer their sacrifice of praise (Heb. 13:15) to the sacrificed Victim of the Passover.

Of all the Gospel accounts, John's narrative especially ties Jesus's death on the cross with Passover and the sacrifice of the Passover lambs (John 19:31, 42). The paschal victim of the enslaved Hebrews was a male lamb without blemish. It was slain on the night before their deliverance from Egypt, and its blood marked them all as God's own protected people when the angel of death passed over the land of their captors (Exod. 12:1–13). The Israelites' entrance into the Promised Land began that night, when the blood of God's chosen sacrifice was spilled and sprinkled upon their doorposts.

Paul writes that Christ is now *our* Passover lamb. "*O salutaris hostia*," Thomas Aquinas wrote in one of his hymns—"O saving Victim, opening wide the door of heaven." Christ's blood protects us from death and destruction and marks our pathway to eternal life.

Thus, the opening praises of Easter do not in any way jump over Christ's sacrificial death. In fact, they begin there. "Look at my hands and my feet," said the risen Jesus to his disciples (Lk. 24:39). The Victor's body still bore the Victim's wounds.

Take some time in prayer today to offer your praises to Jesus —for his resurrection and for his death.

Wednesday of Easter Week

READ JOHN 1:29–32

The next day [John the Baptist] saw Jesus coming toward him
and declared, "Here is the Lamb of God
who takes away the sin of the world!"
—John 1:29

"The lamb has redeemed the sheep:
The innocent Christ has reconciled sinners to the Father."

Listen.

When the young boy Isaac asked of his father, "Where is the lamb for the burnt offering?" Abraham answered, "God will provide himself the lamb for a burnt offering, my son" (Gen. 22:7–8). The story leads us to believe that, at that moment, Abraham was thinking of his own son as God's "provision." But, when he lifted his knife and the dreadful moment arrived to make good on his promised obedience to God, an alternative sacrifice was provided, and Isaac was spared.

Certainly, as indicated by his teaching, John the Baptist knew his Torah well, and the "sacrifice of Isaac" must have been one of the stories in his mind when he saw Jesus and proclaimed to some of his followers, "Behold, the Lamb of God!" Over the next three years, Jesus would try on numerous occasions to explain to his disciples that it was necessary for him to "lay down his life for the sheep" (John 10:11). But not until he actually did so, and then presented himself alive once again, did they even begin to understand who this Lamb was. (Even then, he found them "slow of heart to believe"—Lk. 24:25–27).

Abraham was right. God did provide a Lamb for the burnt offering—a Lamb, as John told us, who would take away the sin of the world; a Lamb, as *Victimae paschali* reminds us, who would redeem the sheep; a Lamb, as the seer John beheld, who will sit on a throne and reign forever and ever (Rev. 5:6, 12–14).

How does the image of Jesus as the Lamb of God help you appreciate who he is and what he has done for you?

Thursday of Easter Week

Read Romans 6:9

We know that Christ, being raised from the dead, will never die again; death no longer has dominion over him.
—Romans 6:9

"Death and life battle in an amazing duel:
The dead Leader of Life reigns, alive"

Listen.

Christ is risen from the dead, trampling down death by death, and upon those in the tombs bestowing life." This ancient hymn from the Eastern Byzantine church captures well the wondrous and even bewildering paradox of Christ's death and resurrection. Death is defeated by death itself, wrestled down and trampled underfoot. *Mors et vita duello* we sing in the Easter sequence. Listening to it, we hear that the music itself rises in pitch, reaching a height and stress that is repeated only once more, with the concluding proclamation: *Scimus Christum surrexisse*—"We know that Christ is risen!"

For both the East and West, our Easter song is offered in praise of a Warrior-Savior who clandestinely went behind the battle line to encounter his enemy face-to-face. This was no duel (*duello*) at twenty paces. The entire phrase—*duello conflixere mirando*—paints the picture of a violent collision, of hand-to-hand combat. To defeat death, Christ entered the realm of death and returned victorious. If death is a kingdom, it now has a new Ruler who reigns supreme and forever alive, bestowing life upon all of his subjects. "He will wipe away every tear from their eyes. Death will be no more; mourning and crying and pain will be no more, for the first things have passed away" (Rev. 21:4).

Today, we sing the praises of One who has faced death in all of its dark forms, who knows all of its tactics, and who, by actually submitting himself to its power, has rendered it powerless. *Mirando* we sing—amazing!

In whatever form you may be "tasting death" today, can you put your trust in the Victor over death? How will you do that?

Friday of Easter Week

Read John 20:11–18

[Mary Magdalene] bent over to look into the tomb, and she saw two angels in white sitting where the body of Jesus had been lying, one at the head and the other at the feet. They said to her, "Woman, why are you weeping?"
—John 20:11b–13a

"Tell us, Mary, what did you see on the way?
'The sepulchre of the living Christ,
and I saw the glory of the Risen One:
The angel witnesses, The head cloth and the clothing.'"

Listen.

Today, we come to a change of tone in the Easter sequence. Up to this point, lifting out a series of biblical images having to do with Christ's resurrection, the piece has been like a high-spirited hymn, to be joyfully declaimed by a choir or even an entire congregation. But with the words *Dic nobis Maria*, we are asked to take a pause in the celebration and listen in on a brief dialogue. A new voice is added.

Imagine that the choir has been walking along a street just outside Jerusalem, singing the news that Jesus is alive once again, and calling upon others to join them in their happy song. They round a corner and come upon Mary Magdalene. Realizing that they now have a firsthand witness before them, they ask the question we can imagine she heard a hundred times that week: "Tell us, Mary, what did you see?" "I saw . . . " she answers. Given the imagery of these brief lines, it's easy to see how *Victimae paschali laudes* would, in time, evolve into something more theatrical, even expanding into what we now know of as Passion plays.

Mary Magdalene's answer in the Easter sequence is a compilation of her "testimony" taken from all four Gospel accounts. For her role as a reliable witness and as the first messenger of the Resurrection (other than the angels!), she is honored by Christians around the world and has even been referred to as the "apostle to the apostles."

Imagine yourself in Mary Magdalene's place on Easter morning.
Walk through the events of the morning that she experienced.
What stands out for you?

Saturday of Easter Week

Read Mark 16:1–7

"But go, tell his disciples and Peter that he is going ahead of you to Galilee; there you will see him, just as he told you."
—Mark 16:7

"Christ my hope has risen:
He is preceding His own to Galilee.
We know the Christ has truly risen from the Dead:
Conquerer King, be merciful to us."

Listen.

Today completes the octave of Easter, those days bathed in the immediate glow of the Resurrection in which *Victimae paschali laudes* serves as the primary Easter chant. Before concluding with one last choral announcement—"We know that Christ has truly risen!"—the final phrase is given to Mary Magdalene. Mary's words are both a confession of her trust in the risen Christ and a message of comfort to Jesus's mourning and confused disciples.

In naming Christ as her "hope," she sums up all that she has come to believe about him. In passing on the message about Jesus's wish to meet his disciples, she is saying something about what he believes about them. For what does it say when one of the first things Jesus wants to do after his resurrection is to get together with the same men who deserted him, even denied him? The answer to that question lies at the heart of the Lent–Easter message, and we will always be grateful to Mary for passing the message on to Jesus's followers. To all of us.

"Remember that you are dust, and to dust you shall return." / "Alleluia! Christ is risen! The Lord is risen indeed! Alleluia!" Though as liturgical words their use is separated by nearly seven weeks, as truths of the Christian life these two phrases sound in unison within us every day. What holds them together? *Miserere* we prayed on Ash Wednesday (the opening word of Psalm 51), and *Miserere* we pray today (the final word of the Easter Sequence). Jesus Christ is the mercy of God in flesh and blood, which is why we give thanks. For his mercy endures forever.

Looking back over the past eight weeks, what are some of the things you have learned from these chant pieces?

Save us, Lord, while we keep vigil; keep us while we sleep, that we may watch with Christ and rest in peace.

—*Compline antiphon*

ACKNOWLEDGMENTS

Audio chants are taken from the following recordings by Gloriæ Dei Cantores Schola.

Gregorian Requiem: Chants of the Requiem Mass

The Chants of Transfiguration

The Beloved Son

I am With You

The Chants of Easter

Chant transcriptions are taken from GregoBase (gregobase.selapa.net).

ABOUT PARACLETE PRESS

PARACLETE PRESS IS THE PUBLISHING ARM of the Cape Cod Benedictine community, the Community of Jesus. Presenting a full expression of Christian belief and practice, we reflect the ecumenical charism of the Community and its dedication to sacred music, the fine arts, and the written word.

SCAN TO READ MORE

Learn more about us at our website:
www.paracletepress.com
or phone us toll-free at 1.800.451.5006

MORE GREGORIAN CHANT
FROM GLORIAE DEI CANTORES SCHOLA

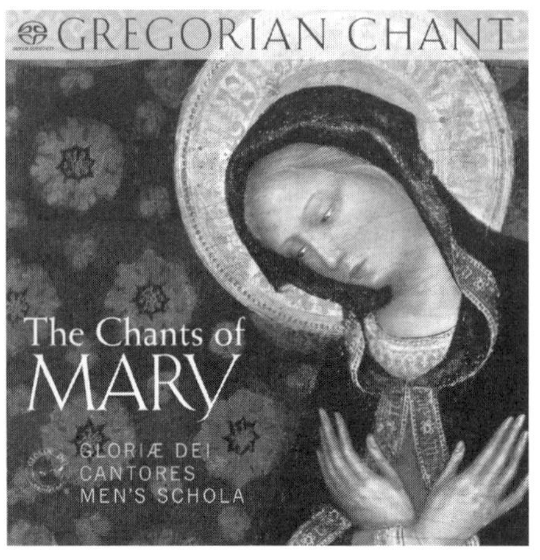

LEARNING MORE ABOUT GREGORIAN CHANT

THE SONG OF PRAYER

A beginner's guide to the singing and understanding of Gregorian chant.

REFLECTIONS ON THE SPIRITUALITY OF GREGORIAN CHANT

A lively and lovely book by Dom Jacques Hourlier on the spiritual aspects of chant.

2025 First Printing

Christ in Our Midst: Daily Lenten Reflections Through Scripture & Gregorian Chant

ISBN 979-8-89348-028-3

Library of Congress Cataloging-in-Publication Data
Names: Paraclete Press compiler | Gloriae Dei Cantores. Schola compiler
Title: Christ in our midst : daily Lenten reflections through scripture and Gregorian chant / Paraclete Press and Gloriae Dei Cantores Schola.
Description: Brewster, Massachusetts : Paraclete Press, [2025] | Summary: "A Lenten daily devotional featuring 40 days of Gregorian chant in Latin and English, coupled with Scripture readings and interactive prompts for personal contemplation and worship"-- Provided by publisher.
Identifiers: LCCN 2025016214 | ISBN 9798893480283 (hardcover)
Subjects: LCSH: Lent--Prayers and devotions | Gregorian chants | BISAC: RELIGION / Holidays / Easter & Lent | RELIGION / Christian Living / Prayer
Classification: LCC BV85 .C498 2025 | DDC 242/.34--dc23/eng/20250505
LC record available at https://lccn.loc.gov/2025016214
10 9 8 7 6 5 4 3 2 1

Published by Paraclete Press
Brewster, Massachusetts
www.paracletepress.com

Printed in India